THE HUMANE GARDENER

THE
HUMANE
GARDENER

Nurturing a Backyard Habitat
FOR WILDLIFE

Nancy Lawson

Princeton Architectural Press *New York*

To the two gentlest souls I know:

my late dog Mattiebo, who introduced me to
the wonders of our yard that my duller human senses
could not have perceived on their own,

and my husband, Will Heinz, who treats all living
creatures—human, animal, and plant—
with the kindness and dignity they deserve.

Published by Princeton Architectural Press
A McEvoy Group company
37 East 7th Street, New York, New York 10003
202 Warren Street, Hudson, New York 12534
www.papress.com

Editor: Sara Stemen Designer: Benjamin English
Developmental editor: Simone Kaplan-Senchak

Special thanks to: Janet Behning, Nicola Brower, Abby Bussel,
Erin Cain, Tom Cho, Barbara Darko, Jenny Florence,
Jan Cigliano Hartman, Lia Hunt, Mia Johnson, Valerie Kamen,
Diane Levinson, Jennifer Lippert, Kristy Maier, Sara McKay,
Eliana Miller, Jaime Nelson Noven, Esme Savage, Rob Shaeffer,
Paul Wagner, and Joseph Weston of Princeton Architectural Press
—Kevin C. Lippert, publisher

Library of Congress Cataloging-in-Publication Data
NAMES: Lawson, Nancy, 1970– author.
TITLE: The humane gardener : nurturing a backyard habitat
for wildlife / Nancy Lawson.
OTHER TITLES: Nurturing a backyard habitat for wildlife
DESCRIPTION: First edition. | New York : Princeton Architectural
Press, [2017] | Includes bibliographical references.
IDENTIFIERS: LCCN 2016029007 | ISBN 9781616895549 (alk. paper)
SUBJECTS: LCSH: Gardening to attract wildlife. | Garden ecology.
CLASSIFICATION: LCC QL59 .L395 2017 | DDC 577.5/54—dc23
LC record available at https://lccn.loc.gov/2016029007

AUTHOR'S NOTE

Though conventional style guides have long frowned upon the practice, I use gender pronouns when referencing animals—from coyotes to caterpillars—throughout this book. After working for many years as an editor at the Humane Society of the United States, I became so accustomed to it that I wouldn't think of going back. Animals are not inanimate objects, and neither are any of the other living creatures among us, yet we use language to separate ourselves from nonhuman beings. As Robin Wall Kimmerer notes in *Braiding Sweetgrass*,

> Maybe a grammar of animacy could lead us to whole new ways of living in the world, other species a sovereign people, a world with a democracy of species, not a tyranny of one—with moral responsibility to water and wolves, and with a legal system that recognizes the standing of other species. It's all in the pronouns.

INTRODUCTION

I used to make many paths into the garden, but somehow nature always found a way to color outside the lines, foiling my straight-and-narrow routes with unruly stalks and new shoots. I would yank her additions out, relocate them, and whine to myself about such encroachments on my prefabricated vision of what a yard should be. It would be years before I understood that while paths through our two-acre plot were arbitrary for us human inhabitants, they were a much-needed escape for other species—the one place where a plant could at least seed, sprout, take hold, and perhaps be noticed instead of mowed down. Early in my gardening journey, these flamboyant wildflowers would have been better off as wallflowers. Unfortunately for the plants and animals who depended on them, each new sign of life was guilty until proven innocent, a threat to the establishment.

One such interloper came in the form of a broad-leaved and thick-stemmed suspect I noticed on my way to work one morning. Daring to inch up in front of our split-rail fence, it looked ominously ready to overtake our property if I didn't act fast. There was no hesitation as I walked past my husband with his power trimmer and issued the death sentence: *Off with his head!*

Less than twenty minutes passed before a roadside sighting of the same species in bloom alerted me to my error and prompted a phoned-in stay of execution. But it was too late. I had casually ordered the ritual decapitation of a plant that, had I only let it, would soon have hosted hundreds of animals: the beautiful but unfortunately named common milkweed.

In retrospect, it's not surprising that my most influential learning experience in horticulture came while sitting at a traffic light next to a neglected ditch at the intersection of a major highway and a nondescript suburban road. Those are the areas where the pretty plants grow and the hungry creatures go. Often listed as preferred habitats of wildflowers, these so-called "waste places" are forgotten spaces, spared temporarily from human interference while we go about our business of tearing nature down elsewhere. They are some of the last areas on our large patch of the planet for our fellow species to colonize and survive.

All my years of consuming mainstream gardening publications and TV shows hadn't prepared me for my milkweed sighting, nor had my Master Gardener training. In fact, even at a time when gardeners around the country are clamoring to plant milkweed species to save the monarch butterfly, who can lay her eggs on nothing else, Maryland's Master Gardener manual still lists this plant as a problematic invader.

By these conventional standards, my property is a disaster. It's now filled with members of wildlife-sustaining species that have been cut down, dug up, sprayed, and otherwise brutalized on this continent for decades, sometimes centuries. It's home to any animal who wants to make a life here and refuge to others just passing through. Only two things are unwelcome: chemicals and invasive vegetation known to supplant wildlife habitat. Everyone else, from smartweed to milkweed, from ground beetles to groundhogs, has an open invitation.

The guest list, of course, wasn't always so inclusive. Before my milkweed revelation, I was an unwittingly graceless host to many other species, once aiming a hose at a mass of ladybug eggs, thinking they were aphids. I ripped out jewelweed, a hummingbird favorite, assuming from its name that it was a trespasser with nefarious intentions. I cut down walnut and hickory saplings, mistaking them for the invasive tree of heaven.

My heart was mostly in the right place, but my head was steeped in the marketing ploys of the Landscaping Industrial Complex, not to mention long-ingrained cultural sentiments that divide the world into endless false dichotomies: beneficial insects versus "pests," acceptable garden plants versus "weeds," order versus chaos. Feeding a multibillion-dollar industry hawking all manner of poisonous potions and outsized tools is a constant stream of cynical advertisements that prey on our insecurities and cater to our basest fears. From their warlike parlance, we learn that animals are out to get us, that plants are messy, that humans reluctant to unleash weapons of mass destruction on denizens of the natural world—especially insects—are freaks of nature themselves.

The attempt to engender fear of other species stretches well beyond negative portrayals of invertebrates. Chemical giants advise destroying all insects in the ground because if you don't, God forbid, you'll "see animals such as skunks and birds visiting your lawn to feed on the grubs." Tree service companies decry the practice of leaving life-saving snags (standing dead trees) because "birds, bees, squirrels, and other pests can seek refuge" in them. Fear-mongering wildlife control operators grasp at straws when trying to persuade home-owners to kill mammals for the crime of mere existence: "Groundhogs are deceptively pleasant-looking creatures with chubby bodies and squatty legs," one popular company warns its customers. "When cornered, however, they are aggressive defenders of their territory, another reason why you're loathe to see one in your yard."[1]

At a time when our fellow inhabitants of the earth increasingly depend on our mercy and ingenuity to survive, our default has instead been to kill and destroy. We live in an era where the artillery of choice is so accessible, the reaction to nature so thoughtless and automatic, that dying bumblebees now fall out of trees by the tens of thousands, poisoned by insecticides for the sake of aesthetics. One-third of native bumblebee species are imperiled, with at least one possibly already extinct. Monarch butterfly numbers in the eastern United States have plummeted by more than 90 percent in two decades. A third of all North American birds—432 species—are at risk of extinction and in need of urgent conservation action. Worldwide, populations of mam-mals, birds, reptiles, amphibians, and fish have declined by 52 per-cent. More than 40 percent of invertebrate pollinators, especially bees and butterflies, are in danger of vanishing from the planet, too.[2]

Among the host of reasons for the losses—habitat destruction, pesticides, climate change, invasive species—the average homeowner holds in his or her hands some of the most reversible: in the United States we've covered with turfgrass more than forty million acres—an area about eight times the size of New Jersey. It's our number one irrigated crop. On these virtual monocultures, we spray tens of millions of pounds of pesticides each year, harming countless animals.[3] We plant species known to invade habitat, displacing essential food and shelter for wildlife. We remove every uninvited plant that could harbor a butterfly in the making, every stump that could give shade and moisture to a toad, every seed head that could nourish a goldfinch during cold winter days.

What happens when we stop? When we spare even the smallest creatures from our sharp blades and stultifying intentions? When we let the fallen leaves be and the decaying logs lie? When we reject the dominant paradigm of three-shrubs-per-acre of suburban lawn? What if we could learn to see the world from the perspective of other species, both plant and animal, and understand that they, too, deserve the chance to make a life here?

It might look a little like the property of Dennis Mudd, who rejected the American dream of palm trees and expansive lawns in his gated California community by creating a native plant garden of extraordinary beauty, or like the diverse wetland of Loret Setters, whose land outside her Florida mobile home is teeming with uncommon animal species that moved in only after she put down the power tools and let nature take over. It could resemble Charlotte Adelman's urban backyard woodland and community prairie, where pesticides are banished and holes in leaves are cause for celebration—a sure sign that animals have found the host plants she added especially for their young. Or it could be a kind of mini-wildlife rehabilitation center like that of Jennifer Howard in Ontario, where ever-encroaching development has made life more dangerous for animals just trying to cross the road from one habitat fragment to another.

A humane garden feeds animals of all kinds but can also be a feast for human eyes. Here, cutleaf coneflower, joe-pye weed, and yucca sustain butterflies, bees, moths, and other pollinators, while a fountain provides water for birds.

A garden planted to meet the needs of species beyond ourselves could even take the form of a farm like that of Tammi Hartung, who grows enough for her family while also sharing the bounty with her wild friends in Colorado. And it should always honor the dead, like the many fallen leaves and moss- and lichen-covered logs providing rich habitat in Oregon landscape designer Eileen Stark's backyard sanctuary.

These humane gardeners embody the ethic of compassionate landscaping, challenging long-held assumptions about animals, plants, and themselves. Their efforts are an inspiration, proof that our species can do infinitely more good by helping nature along rather than snuffing it out—on any property and a range of budgets. A growing body of research validates their efforts, revealing the importance of such home gardens to pollinator diversity and demonstrating the power of native plants to sustain many more animals than the typical suburban yard.

Because our continent is vast and diverse, there's no single prescription for creating habitat for wildlife. But the tenets of nurturing a humane backyard are universal, and learning to follow them is about unlearning and having the courage to question everything you thought you knew about gardening. In my own yard, I still make mistakes, usually when I've listened to a so-called expert instead of my own heart. My garden's not perfect, and neither are the gardens of the people profiled in this book. But that's part of the point. Perfection is a human construct, a poor substitute for the natural exuberance and resiliency that make a house a home—not just for us, but for all species. The cavity-nesting bees would certainly be happier if we didn't cut down dead stalks where they could lay their eggs, and the birds would approve if we didn't scoop up the leaves and all the tasty seeds and insects hiding there. We don't have to control everything, and we can't anyway. So why not give nature a try?

Why import habitat-destroying plants from overseas when we have gorgeous natives that provide a feast for our eyes and for animal bellies? In Maryland, blooms of coral honeysuckle (above left), cardinal flower (above right), and cutleaf coneflower (left) beckon bees, hummingbirds, and butterflies. As the seasons change, blooms of American beautyberry (below right) and possumhaw viburnum (below left) give way to berries nourishing hungry birds and other wildlife.

CHAPTER 1

A New Kind of Dream Home: Plant Native Plants

───────────

More than mere decoration, plants are the foundation of any humane garden.

As a young homeowner with visions of a paradise of perpetual bloom, I was the perfect target. Taunted by gardening magazines exploding with color and texture, I devoured the glossy spreads of picture-perfect flowers, Romanesque fountains, and foliage-draped trellises melting into a lush suburban dreamscape.

Though my husband teased me about my addiction to "flower porn," I also read these publications for the articles, learning about everything from proper spacing of tomato transplants to the best time to trim back dead perennial stalks. But inspiration eventually turned into frustration, and it became clear that Will had a point about the emptiness of the endeavor.

There were many rules to follow but not much heart behind them. I learned how to start seeds but not why I should leave their progeny—the seed heads—in place as a food source for birds. I developed an almost innate sense of how to keep voluptuous cottage garden flowers thriving but had little knowledge of trees, shrubs, and other plants critical to wildlife. Most wasteful of all, I looked beyond my borders for beauty, rather than taking the time to understand the potential already there in my own backyard.

Plant wanderlust is ingrained in our culture and in my family. My father sold tuberous begonias—species native to tropical and subtropical climates—from a greenhouse behind his Oregon home when he was ten, a precursor to a career that included traveling overseas in search of exotic species for the floral industry. Along with necklaces, dolls, and chocolates for us kids, he brought home fascinating plant souvenirs like Australia's aptly named kangaroo paw, which claimed a revered spot on the kitchen table of my childhood.

Horticulturists have been enraptured with such novelties for centuries, importing and breeding them largely for their decorative value. Some species have become treasured and well-behaved heirlooms beloved by both humans and animals. But others, growing out of context and without their natural controls, pose significant threats to wildlife habitats; about a third of the vegetation in local woodlots and fields is now nonnative, and 85 percent of invasive species were introduced by the horticultural trade.[1]

In spite of all we know in hindsight, old habits die hard. As my father and I have embraced the trend toward gardening with more wildlife-friendly plants, we've watched with puzzlement a backlash from those who characterize native plant advocates as "extremist" or, as I heard one professor say, "xenophobic." But perhaps it shouldn't be a surprise. We are a nation of immigrants who eradicated many of the land's previous inhabitants—the humans, plants, and animals alike— and dispensed with most of what they had to teach us. Ken Parker, a horticulturist and member of the Seneca Nation, has spent his career trying to bring some of them back. "I'm not a plant racist. I love all plants," he says. "But our plants are in the minority now—we need to do something about that. We should be able to drive down the road and see a shrubby St. John's wort or an American hazelnut, [or look at] the landscaping at the airport in Denver and see Rocky Mountain pines. I don't, I see burning bush. I see the same thing over and over."

Native plants were once everything to Parker's people—providing food, shelter, and medicine—but "we've kind of lost that now that all of us have become more urbanized," he says. Parker sees the evidence everywhere and does what he can to reverse the damage: Hearing at a Seneca Nation meeting that hundreds of Dutch bulbs were about to be ordered for median strips, he suggested native grasses and fruiting shrubs in their place. Arriving at a sugar mapling workshop at a community center flanked by invasive Norway maples, he made a pitch to replace them with native sugar maples. At Native-run casinos, he pointed out the incongruity of buildings decorated with Native American artwork on the inside and European plants outdoors.

Keenly aware of the devastating consequences for wildlife, Parker is also pained by the effects of misguided landscaping on our own species. At a time when mounting research shows the power of nature to calm our moods, help us focus, and improve our mental health,[2] we continue to take our plants for granted. Aiming to instill more reverence for their role in our lives, Parker was instrumental in implementing a Seneca Nation policy of using only indigenous species in new landscaping of public spaces, the first of its kind among US Native nations. It's also why he started the Food Is Our Medicine project, which highlights cooking with traditional plants as a way to combat the high incidence of heart disease, diabetes, and obesity within Native communities. People are healthier when they have access to natural foods, Parker believes, just as trees, bushes, and flowers thrive when growing in the soil and sun conditions they need.

Gardening for the good of people and wildlife does not signal hatred toward invasive Asian burning bush and English ivy, as some reductionist narratives would have us believe; all plants have value somewhere, and ecologists worldwide contend with introduced species that are out of sync with their surroundings. Even a quick walk through my property reveals a mirror image of the problem: Japanese barberries that are kept in balance by the soil and climate conditions of their homeland have few such restrictions in our woods, where they seed all the way into the stream bank. On the other hand, the broomsedge that threatens habitat in Japan and Australia grows companionably here in our meadow, where it serves as an early successional species in restoring old pastureland. Both these species provide food and cover for wildlife in their native ranges, and both wreak havoc on local ecology elsewhere.

As I wage a halfhearted battle with barberry and other invaders that ended up here through no fault of their own, I often wish I could hold an international plant exchange with gardeners overseas, together reversing the sins of our horticultural past in whatever small way we can. A simple handoff is impossible, of course, as is a return to the way things were. But we do have the capacity to improve the habitat in our own backyards, and to reject the American dream of lush lawns and exotic plants for what it really is—a nightmare for animals—in favor of a new paradigm, one that takes its cue from how plants grow in the wild.

The following principles, modeled on nature's time-tested recipes, can bring abundant life to any garden through native plantings.

Plant for all seasons and sizes.

When the continent was still teeming with a diversity of species, animals could find sustenance throughout the year; in fact, many plants in turn evolved to depend on them for it. Mayapple, a shade-lover that blooms in spring, relies on box turtles for seed dispersal. Yuccas can't live without yucca moths, who transfer pollen among plants before laying eggs in the summer flowers, where larvae hatch and eat some of the prolific seeds. Squash bees pollinate squash blossoms as if their lives depended on them—because they do; they're among the many specialist bee species that forage on pollen only from plants of certain lineages.

Bees with broader palates also need blooms from early spring to late autumn. If a queen bumblebee emerges from her overwintering site in the leaf litter and finds little but turfgrass, she'll have a hard time gathering enough pollen and nectar to start a new colony. If a monarch doesn't have swaths of goldenrod, asters, and other late-flowering plants lighting her fall migration path, she may run out of fuel.[3]

A variety of flower shapes also draws diverse diners. Hummingbird moths unfurl their long proboscises to reach deep into the narrow corollas of spring-blooming woodland phlox and the midsummer blossoms of wild bergamot. Long-tongued bees access nectar from deep flowers like columbine and penstemon, while short-tongued bees need more open blooms.[4]

A succession of flowers, fruits, and seed heads can help ensure no one goes hungry. To make the task of converting to wildlife-friendly plants less daunting, Parker recommends starting with a dozen native wildflower species—four for each season of bloom—and adding a

Early-flowering plants like Virginia bluebells (left) welcome bees in spring when little else is blooming yet. Late-season blooms like those of blue mist-flower (above) are lifesavers for skippers and other insects still looking for food when many plants have finished flowering.

The tubular flowers of wild bergamot are the perfect size for the long proboscises of hummingbird moths. The more open blooms of native dogwoods and viburnums feed mining bees, syrphid flies, and other tiny pollinators. Swamp milkweed creates an easy perching and dining spot for bumblebees, beetles, and many other pollinators.

few grasses, some fruiting shrubs, and two nut-bearing trees. You can even feed yourself in the process, since many natives—including paw-paws, blueberries, prickly pears, and elderberries—satisfy the taste buds of both wildlife and people.

Add foundation plants for animals.

Mainstream horticulture has long treated leaves and grasses as a the-atrical backdrop: chartreuse groundcover creates a complementary color scheme and grasses add a focal point, we're told, while hedges of evergreen shrubs enhance winter interest. But the obsession with ornamental foliage and evergreen "foundation" plantings overshadow

Layered borders can include native vines that feed and shelter wild-life. Coral honeysuckle, an easy-to-maintain vine native to much of the eastern United States, provides nectar, berries, and a dense growth habit for nesting.

Grasses have long been treated as theatrical back-drops or "focal points" in the garden. But river oats and many others feed the caterpillars of butterflies like this northern pearly-eye, who perhaps not coincidentally showed up after I added a substantial number of native grasses to my garden. Warm-season species, including little bluestem, Indiangrass, switchgrass, and prairie dropseed, also provide habitat for grass-land birds.

the truly foundational role of native leaves in the food web. Most plant-eating insects—who are themselves a dietary staple for birds and other animals—eat only species they coevolved with, not the forsythia, tulip bulbs, and Japanese hollies found at the local big-box center.

To create borders that benefit wildlife, add native trees and shrubs like arborvitae and hollies and semi-evergreen vines such as coral honeysuckle. Plant deciduous hedges in layers, mixing shrubs, grasses, and wildflowers that can provide food and cover for birds in winter and privacy for you.

Triage the removal of invaders.

If you're faced with a large lawn and an encroaching tangle of invasive species, it's easy to get overwhelmed. Replace at your own pace, removing the most prolific spreaders first and planting vigorous natives in their place.

Enlist natives more directly in the standoff by inserting them into patches of invasives—a method I discovered by accident after setting aside transplants of golden ragwort, a native groundcover, near a patch

By inserting just a few transplants of golden ragwort under some sassafras trees, I conscripted the stalwart native groundcover into guerilla warfare against invasive garlic mustard.

of garlic mustard, a nonnative herb encroaching on US and Canadian forests. Emitting chemicals that inhibit the growth of surrounding species, garlic mustard invades the understory and is considered a significant threat to the West Virginia white butterfly, which mistakes it for a safe place to lay eggs. But the plant seems to have met its match in the golden ragwort, which rambled out of its pots and over the invader lurking under our sassafras grove.[5]

Though removing invasives helps wildlife populations in the long term, individual animals can be caught in the crossfire. Plants with dense growth habit, like bush honeysuckle and multiflora rose, often harbor bird nests, and flowering nonnatives like purple dead nettle and dandelions provide sustenance to early spring bees in otherwise denuded landscapes. In some cases, waiting until plants have dropped leaves or passed peak flowering time can prevent short-term harm to the animals who depend on them.

Plant "green" mulch.

No plants are islands, despite the common practice of spacing them too far apart and adding suffocating piles of wood mulch to suppress surrounding vegetation. In the forest, woody plants and herbaceous species grow together in an intricate matrix that looks nothing like our lonely landscapes. "We're not being creative," says Parker, "and we're not utilizing plants like they were meant to be utilized, which is as a self-sustaining system."

Far from being static sculptures, plants change over time and in ways not always seen aboveground. Some are the first to soak up sun and radiate flowers in early spring, going dormant just as the species above them spring to life and cast shade over their domains. Some send deep roots into the soil, while their neighbors move more laterally near the surface. And though a number of plants are party animals that quickly multiply, others are introverts, growing singly or with just a few of their kind.

Switchgrass is one of many species that grow naturally among ground-covering neighbors, but gardeners often plant it in isolation. "That leaves a lot of gaps open between these tall, beautiful plants that in the wild would be filled with these other species," says Claudia West, an ecological designer and the coauthor of *Planting in a Post-Wild World*. "And if these gaps are open, it's an open invitation for weeds."

Rather than using wood mulch that needs to be repeatedly replenished to suppress those weeds, imitate natural growth patterns by adding sedges, grasses, and native groundcovers as "green mulch" among taller plants. The more complex root systems of these intermingling species will help heal compacted soil, improve stormwater filtration, and nurture microorganisms that are critical to a healthy soil community. The low leaf canopy will provide food and shelter for many species, giving rabbits a place to nest, toads a safe spot for overwintering, and birds a year-round feast of insects.

Trade cultivars for straight species.

A rose by any other name—or a holly or sunflower, for that matter—is sometimes not even recognizable to wildlife. Every year I watch the orange fruits of a winterberry holly I bought specifically for birds wither untouched on their branches, while the redder fruits of neighboring winterberries get stripped clean. Twice I've made the mistake of buying sunflower seeds to grow for pollinators, only to discover

Instead of bark mulch, use native groundcovers as "green mulch." The ragwort not only crowds out invasives under these chokeberries; it also negates the need to weed, feeds small pollinators in early spring, and creates a rich layer where birds can forage and rabbits can nest undisturbed.

Heirloom annual flowers can help fill in seasonal gaps for insects and birds while you continue to add more native plants. Sunflowers are easy to grow from seed, but look for tried-and-true varieties to avoid adding plants with the pollen bred out of them.

Around and around a modern hybrid rose went this sweat bee in my garden, searching haplessly for sustenance before finally abandoning the mission. Just yards away, a syrphid fly was having more luck on a Virginia rose baring its reproductive parts for all pollinators to see.

they'd been bred to be pollenless. One recent summer I watched bees try in vain to access rose nectar made inaccessible by an unnatural extravagance of petals.

These hybrids and cultivars—species variants grown for particular qualities such as larger blooms, smaller growth, altered leaf colors, or double petals—can obscure or even eliminate the resources wildlife need most: pollen and nectar sources, edible berries, accessible flower shapes, and digestible foliage. Even when plants do offer nutritional value, alterations may confuse animals who use visual and other sensory cues to locate food.

Not all native plant cultivars are fruitless, so to speak; ongoing research reveals mixed results, with some proving productive for pollinators and caterpillars.[6] But you can't go wrong by purchasing unmanipulated species (often referred to as "straight species") grown the way nature intended. Unlike cultivars, which are usually reproduced clonally, straight species are genetically diverse, keeping plant populations more resilient. To grow them, consult with native plant nurseries in your region; if they are difficult to find, consider planting some of your own from seed.

Don't love your plants to death. While it's logical to replenish nutrients in fields cultivated for quick-growth vegetable and grain crops, applying strict agricultural regimens to home landscapes can be deadly to certain species. What we perceive as poor soil is sometimes exactly what natives like purple lovegrass and dense blazing star prefer. Fertilizer and excessive compost can reduce their vigor, lead to weed outbreaks, and even kill plants better left alone. "They are just totally exhausted and overwhelmed by the

Liatris, one of many native plants that prefer not to be coddled, may not survive long in nutrient-rich soils. As you convert your landscape to these more wildlife-friendly species, help your neighbors understand your goals by posting an informative sign. Organizations offering them include the Xerces Society for Invertebrate Conservation, the Humane Society of the United States, the National Wildlife Federation, state native plant societies, and community watershed-protection programs.

nutrients that they would never find in a natural environment," says West. "We don't trust plants enough."

Overwatering is also a common problem, especially in drought-stricken regions like California, where some gardeners are converting their landscapes from thirsty exotics to indigenous species. Accustomed to artificially irrigating, they risk destroying a critical partnership between soil microorganisms and plants. In one of nature's many fascinating mutualistic relationships, fungi in the soil take up carbohydrates from native plant roots in exchange for guarding those roots against pathogens and serving as a kind of water and nutrient reservoir. Given too many inputs, the balance breaks down: plants treat their former fungal friends as parasites, pathogens move in, and the whole system can collapse.[7]

The negative response of these native plants to our traditional horticultural practices, combined with the sparse presence of natives in the landscape, can lead to a mistaken impression of fragility. But their absence is due only to our propensity to plant species from elsewhere—and to our lack of understanding about what native plants need (and don't need) when we do invite them into the garden. Many are even more lush than their tropical, imported counterparts and, when planted in the right spot, don't just survive but thrive. Unless you live on a former Superfund site or in a development scraped clean of topsoils, species indigenous to your region will know how to grow there; they did so long before anyone came along with a bag of fertilizer and a hose.

In Maryland, my dad has carved out a large patch of his front lawn for a wildflower garden so prolific he now has more milkweed than I do. Across the continent, Dennis Mudd made a similar choice, converting his once lifeless, artificial landscape into one that mimics nature. Nature has signaled her approval, sending snakes, bees, hummingbirds, and coyotes slithering and buzzing and quietly pitter-pattering to a welcoming committee of plants their ancestors knew by instinct and by heart.

Dennis Mudd

entrepreneur and philanthropist

THE HOME

*A two-acre suburban lot and five-acre adjacent
canyon in Poway, California*

Cleveland sage and more than two dozen other species provide nectar for hummingbirds in Dennis Mudd's garden, where bees are also abundant.

A centuries-old mission manzanita tree feeds coyotes and other wildlife.

Painted scenes from around the world decorate the walls of Dennis Mudd's living room: a Vietnamese man in a raggedy army hat, three Maasai boys in the foreground of Mount Kilimanjaro, two of his own sons in the Mediterranean Sea off the coast of Egypt, his wife, Pamela, on a bike behind him in Namibia.

Just outside the room's glass doors, Mudd's artwork celebrating distant places gives way to a space with ties decidedly closer to home. Instead of the exotic palm trees dotting the other properties on the street, native buckwheat and sagebrush thrive on south-facing slopes, an environment they've adapted to over thousands of years. California fuchsias, monkeyflowers, and southern honeysuckle beckon hummingbirds to their tubular blooms. Mission manzanitas, indigenous primarily to San Diego County and Baja California, offer up berries to coyotes; one of the trees on Mudd's land has likely been doing so for centuries. "This is my favorite plant," says Mudd, pointing out the beauty of its purple-red bark. "This one could be five hundred years old since it last burned. And even when they burn, they burn down to the base and then they come back up again."

Mudd's reverence for the plants is not lessened by the knowledge that they didn't travel far to get here. If anything, it makes him appreciate them even more. Maybe that's because turning his house into a home for other species has been an epic journey in itself. In a region overtaken by lawns, Mudd had to become a pioneering botanist in his own backyard.

Like many of his neighbors, Mudd once lived among the traditional trappings of the California dream—palm trees plopped into seas of turfgrass. "I don't think I ever saw an animal here," he says. "Almost no birds."

Feeling no more welcome in the sterile environment than other species did, he frequently escaped on his bike, where he found the hills alive with plants he couldn't yet name. "I gradually fell in love with the nature in the area," he says, "and I decided I wanted to bring it home with me."

The natural beauty of Rattlesnake Canyon, where Mudd often rides his bike, was one of the inspirations for restoring his own land with indigenous species.

Once an illusion of paradise devoid of animals (right and below), Dennis and Pamela Mudd's former concrete-and-palm-tree backyard (above) is now filled with native plants that provide shelter and food for countless creatures.

Twelve years later, surrounded by hundreds of vines, trees, shrubs, and flowers indigenous to the area, Mudd finds beauty not just in the obvious but in the shape of things to come. Walking around his property on a late November day just before the winter rainy season, he points with wonder at the gnarled, ropy wood of an older buckwheat that will soon burst into bloom. He admires the coral-like yellow bush penstemon that appears practically dead but will be covered in large yellow flowers next month. He revels in the scent of white sage leaves and extols the white-flowering currant as the best smell he's ever inhaled from a blossom. He eagerly anticipates the sprouting of the beautiful silver windmill-like seeds from his San Diego mountain mahoganies and the fairy-dancer blooms of his fuchsia-flowering gooseberries.

Mudd's knowledge of each plant's response to its environment is so detailed he can even catalog the changing leaf structure of one of his favorite species, hoaryleaf ceanothus, through the seasons. But though he knows practically every inch of this space, the land still keeps Mudd guessing. Among its many surprises are at least a hundred bright purple showy penstemons that appeared on their own. "Over time, there gets to be a seed bank, and with different sorts of rainfalls, particularly in wet years or unusual years," he says, "you'll see plants start to come out that have never grown [before]."

The path toward a true San Diego sanctuary proved more convoluted than Mudd anticipated. A landscaper hired in 2004 to plant natives installed species of South African and Australian origin. A second company claiming to specialize in natives added plants that

California poppies grow near a spot where the Mudds play boccie.

True to its name, showy penstemon (above) announced its presence in fabulous fashion, sprouting by the hundreds where Mudd had never planted it. Mudd revels in the scent of white sage (right), which attracts a diversity of bees and birds.

The fruit of hollyleaf redberry, which grows on slopes and prefers to receive no supplementary water once established, is an important food source for birds.

Red bush monkeyflower and chalk dudleya both attract hummingbirds. Chalk dudleya is one of many species in the San Diego region with a unique niche, preferring to grow at a slight angle on slopes. If it's planted facing straight up, standing water on the leaves could kill it.

grow hundreds of miles north. Most died. "A 'California native' is kind of a ridiculous concept," says Mudd, "because something that grows in the Bay Area or the Central Coast might as well be in Europe compared to the stuff that grows down in Southern California."

After so much trial and error, there was only one thing left for an entrepreneur like Mudd to do: he took on the project himself. As the founder of two digital music companies, he was no stranger to challenges. He researched plants endemic to the Poway area, took a class in horticulture, and started a website to catalog his findings.

Along the way, he learned that the region's native plants don't thrive on the type of care many gardeners are used to providing. Water helps them get started, but too much of it, especially during the dry season, can ruin intricate relationships between soil organisms and roots. Elevation shifts so quickly that species growing in one area may be doomed even a mile away. "It's just always about growing the right stuff in the right place," Mudd says. "If you grow a plant that needs great drainage on something that's flat, they're not going to do as well."

San Diego County's seemingly harsh environment of endless sun and rock has contributed to the region's rich biodiversity; a greater diversity of plants grows here than in any other county in the continental United States. That's because when conditions are mild and consistent across a landscape, Mudd explains, a few species can spread and dominate. But in the area around his home—which includes his original lot and an adjacent canyon the Mudds purchased as a nature preserve—"every plant will get its own little niche where it figured out how to evolve under very tough sorts of circumstances," he says. "There are plants that grow at different elevations, different distances from the ocean, different marine influences."

Young great horned owls thrive in the natural oasis, where a plentiful supply of squirrels and other small mammals encourages raptors to nest.

With the veil of turfgrass removed, the land reveals its own kind of beauty in the golden hue of the dry season. Rattlesnakes have their place at the nature preserve behind the Mudds' home, where the dogs have been trained to avoid them.

The transformation of Mudd's property has been so complete that he wants more people to experience it, so he donated an expanded statewide version of his database to the California Native Plant Society. Called Calscape, the site invites gardeners to access and contribute information about plants endemic to their communities.

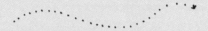

Life begets life here, as raccoons, squirrels, rabbits, gophers, and moles attract hawks, great horned owls, and other raptors to the property. Animals contribute to the very garden that feeds them, planting the seeds of oak trees, sage, buckwheat, and the ceanothus that turns the hillsides bright blue in winter.

Though Mudd uses cages to protect new plantings from dusky-footed woodrats who use vegetation, he's reached a détente with the animals and even finds their tan, sleek coats pretty. Rats' nests aren't "the most pleasing thing in the world," he says, "but they're a part of it all, so I've just learned to accept it."

Rattlesnakes have their place, too, so Mudd's canine clan—two Chesapeake Bay retrievers and a black Lab—have been trained to avoid them, to the point where one "jumped ten feet in the air" upon seeing a snake. The dog pack takes security near the house very seriously, keeping coyotes at a distance, but in the nature preserve and beyond they know it's a free country for all species. "They love to come up here," says Mudd as the dogs play on a rock overlooking the canyon, "but they will never come up here on their own. This is coyote territory. They're very clear about what those borders are."

On warm nights, the Mudds enjoy a magical view from a bench overlooking the canyon. While Anna's hummingbirds put on an aerial show, a colony of bees buzzes behind the pool. Western bluebirds and roadrunners make their appearances, and red-tailed hawks and Cooper's hawks come to feast.

The setting sun casts a golden hue on the plants and lights up tiny insects with a natural sparkle so rare in typical landscapes that Mudd can think only of a fictional reference to describe it. The glow reminds him of the luminescent forest threatened by colonialism and development in the film *Avatar*, he says, as the birds swoop in to catch their tiny prey. In a way, though, Mudd's home represents a kind of chronological inverse of director James Cameron's film—a hopeful postapocalyptic story showing it's still possible to heal a broken land. "It just seems like everything keeps in balance now."

CHAPTER 2

The Beauty of Letting Go:
Let Nature Guide Your Garden

*Partnering with plants and animals brings
a world of discoveries.*

As stormwaters swallowed New Orleans in the aftermath of Hurricane Katrina, I was perusing the rose aisle of a suburban Washington, DC, nursery on my lunch hour. Five years into gardening on our two acres, my husband and I still struggled to make a dent in the never-ending lawn. The task seemed urgent.

By the time I returned to the office, new plants in tow, the Gulf Coast landscape had irreversibly changed. The storm that had initially spared much of the Big Easy left disaster in its surging wake. Levees had been breached, and homes submerged. On vanishing rooftops, people clutching babies, dogs, and cats prayed for rescue from the polluted waters and unforgiving sun.

My colleagues and I at the Humane Society of the United States, where I worked at the time, hastily created a disaster recovery center to reunite devastated pet owners and their animals. For six months our hearts shattered under the weight of lovingly reported details about those we could not find: the slightly limping Lab with a pin in her right front leg, the cat with a smile-shaped white patch peeking

A single sassafras that sprouted on its own has turned into a grove near our patio, mingling with Virginia creeper (above). Both species provide fruit and foliage for birds and caterpillars, including those of the spicebush swallowtail butterfly (top). After the larvae pupate, adults enjoy nectar from bee balm a few feet away (right).

out from her belly, the mastiff who refused to budge from his bed and was too heavy to carry as the waters rose.

Most other things in life, including my garden, began to seem trivial. Learning of storm victims' joy at watching sunflowers sprout from muddy cars in the weeks following the hurricane, I saw my efforts to mold my land in the image of some cultural fantasy as extravagant. I no longer cared how my yard looked and even wondered whether I belonged there at all.

To my surprise, the more I let go, the more the land gave way to real grace. In my neglected flower garden, a volunteer sassafras tree, a host for spicebush swallowtail butterflies, grew into a grove. Berry-laden Virginia creeper vines inched their way over fences and walls, beckoning birds and Pandora sphinx moth caterpillars to feast. Boneset, heath aster, common evening primrose, goldenrods, and other species beloved by bees showed up unannounced and bloomed wherever they planted themselves.

Even the pokeweed returned. It was a plant I'd first met five years earlier, when it dared to pop up on our newly purchased property in the early 2000s. Though struck by the beauty of its hot pink stems and deep purple berries, I couldn't help but feel it didn't belong back then. And that's because it didn't—not at that time, when the only plants in our entire backyard were a lone forsythia bush, two ash trees, and a raggedy little rosebush, plopped down randomly amid a sea of poison-soaked turfgrass. Those didn't belong either—nothing was in its place because there was little nature left.

But I would have been happy to find a reason to keep this gorgeous interloper I couldn't yet name. Turning to the issue of *Organic Gardening* I'd just received, I was excited to see photos of the mystery plant. Unfortunately for the pokeweed and its faunal fans, the species wasn't being highlighted for its virtues. The article's central message was clear: *Rip it out! Now, before it takes over everything, ruthlessly and in short order!* Over the next few years, I dutifully murdered pokeweed wherever I saw it, pulling, digging, and cutting its roots, out of a panic that if I let it go even a little bit, it would swallow us whole by the end of summer.

After learning that bluebirds love pokeweed berries, I felt betrayed by my trusty gardening sources. When I finally decided to give poke-weed a chance during that season following Hurricane Katrina, it didn't disappoint. Belying its reputation as aggressive, it played nice with the other natives I intentionally cultivated, spreading only when filling a void where little else grew.

As a born-again pokeweed proselytizer, I would soon find pas-sionate allies: the Arkansas man who used its berries for ink in the 1930s, the Alabamans who hold festivals to celebrate a salad made from its young shoots, and the New England ecologist who appre-ciates the whole plant for the same reasons I do. Though toxic to humans, the berries feed foxes, squirrels, opossums, raccoons, and many birds; the flowers nourish hummingbirds and tiny pollinators; and the leaves fortify giant leopard moth caterpillars.

Despite pokeweed's many detractors, a growing body of science demonstrates how much fall-migrating birds depend on it and other native plants. Comparing the composition of their berries with that of invasive species along the East Coast, ornithologist Susan Smith Pagano has found that the natives are much higher in the nutri-ents birds need on their long journeys south in the fall. "Smaller birds—passerines—only fly at night, and so every morning they

A host plant for the giant leopard moth, pokeweed also feeds small pollinators like syrphid flies and migrating birds, who rely on its berries to fuel their long autumn journeys.

must find somewhere to set down, be it to rest or to really rapidly replenish their fat stores," says Pagano, an associate professor at the Rochester Institute of Technology, "and they want to do this in a matter of days."

A landscape filled with exotics that carry little nutritional value could spell trouble for their continued journeys. The watery, low-energy berries of imported plants may act as a kind of "nutritional trap," luring birds with cues such as color or abundance but offering little in return. European buckthorn and Asian nandina can even make them sick. "Just because a bird eats something doesn't mean it's good for it," says Pagano. "We eat junk food sometimes. Sometimes birds do the same thing."

Guided by the research of Pagano and other scientists, we can now help birds clean up their diets by modifying our plantings. Along with pokeweed, some of nature's power foods for migratory birds include Virginia creeper, blueberry, serviceberry, elderberry, dogwoods, viburnums, spicebush, black raspberry, bayberry, and winterberry—all species that would rise up on their own if we cut the mowers and gave them a chance.[1]

While many are sold at nurseries now, pokeweed is still maligned even by some of my fellow native plant enthusiasts. And none of my neighbors let it grow—not yet. But thanks to the prescient work of the late nature writer Mary Leister, who walked the lands surrounding my home for decades, I know that in the years not long before my house was built, a rumpled, half-starved yellow-bellied sapsucker flew into this community one October and was transformed by a pokeweed patch, eating and sleeping for days. "It was the stupor, the almost comatose state, of utter exhaustion from which he barely roused at long intervals, ate another berry, and sank back into his torpor," Leister wrote in her 1976 book, *Wildlings*.

Soon he was eating caterpillars, mosquitoes, ants, and tree sap, but pokeberries remained his entrée of choice until he was finally made whole again. They saved his life, and I like to think the plants on my property are seeded descendants of that sapsucker's pokeweed patch, destined to nourish many more of his kind in my yard for generations to come.

The world at our feet

My experiences with pokeweed and other surprise guests in the garden made me wonder: Who else could be saved if we stopped imposing our will on the land and let it begin to write its own story? What plants would we find latent in the soil, and what animals might come back to greet them if we let these hidden seeds sprout?

To make discoveries like these, we often hike through far-flung forests and swim in distant seas. The areas nearest to us are rarely the dearest—and all too easy to dismiss as familiar ground. How familiar are we, though, with who eats, sleeps, and breeds among us? The number of organisms in a single acre exceeds the entire human population; a square meter of soil alone may contain millions of insects and other invertebrates. Yet by 2015 we had identified only about two million species across the planet—a small percentage of all that call this place home. Even as scientists predict the loss of up to half the world's species by mid-century, every year brings an average of twenty thousand more discoveries, including a new species of sweat bee found in the heart of New York City in 2010.[2]

Rather than journey overseas to see a tiger in the wild, try heading outside to find these little "tigers" instead. Dining on the same plants as monarchs, tiger milkweed moth caterpillars have evolved to carry the same alarming colors that birds associate with the unpalatable butterflies. The six-spotted tiger beetle preys voraciously on other insects and spiders throughout its life cycle. Eastern tiger swallowtail butterflies congregate by the dozens on flowers of joe-pye weed.

"There are so many overlooked little creatures that are just as interesting in their own right, and we just go past them and don't notice them," says University of Illinois research scientist Jim Nardi, author of *Life in the Soil: A Guide for Naturalists and Gardeners*. Of my small corner of the earth, he notes, "I would be willing to wager that you have one or two new species in your yard."

In 2012 a trustee at the Natural History Museum of Los Angeles County issued a similar bet, challenging entomologists to find a previously unrecorded species outside her home. They did her one better, expanding the search to thirty properties, mostly private yards, and identifying thirty new species in the span of three months. That they were all flies didn't dilute the significance of the discovery, says project leader Emily Hartop, noting their important role in cleaning up our trash and other messes: "Any time you see those insects, they're doing something that's helpful; they're breaking things down."

Though developing such appreciation for our fellow inhabitants doesn't require the trained eyes of an entomologist or botanist, it helps to walk more slowly and feel more acutely the rhythms of nature. To get started on the path to discovery, follow these tips for seeing plants and animals in close-up—while also learning more about the big picture—right in your own backyard.

Get into the "weeds."

The more you plant for animals, the more they'll seed in return. At least half the species in my yard are unexpected gifts, and the treasures mount with every season. Black raspberries, eastern red cedars, hickories, oaks, sea oat grasses—all species that now command high prices at native plant sales—continue to sprout and spread. Once I almost

Often mistaken for poison sumacs, the exotic-looking but native staghorn sumac isn't even in the same genus. Safe to touch and beautiful to look at, the small trees feed three hundred bird species and serve as an emergency food source in the winter. Squirrels and rabbits like the bark, and deer graze on the fruits and stems.

One of the first plants to colonize abandoned fields or disturbed land in the eastern United States, broomsedge provides seed and cover for birds. Caterpillars feed on the grasses, and bees use the plant for nesting material.

bought a fifteen-dollar pot of broomsedge, only to arrive home and realize that I already had an entire field of this beautiful plant I had previously assumed was a weed.

To learn what botanical bounties lie dormant in your yard, leave some areas unmowed and watch what comes next. If you're new to plants, state native plant societies, online plant groups, and county Master Gardener and Master Naturalist programs can help identify natives and confirm suspected invasive species in need of removal.

Walk through your garden at dawn, at dusk, or after a rainstorm, and you'll be sure to find interesting animals you never realized were there—perhaps a bumblebee sleeping under a false sunflower (right) or a hickory horned devil caterpillar emerging for his evening leafy snack (opposite).

Zoom in on magnificence.

Peer under flowers and leaves, and you'll soon see wasps wiping their faces, caterpillars nibbling away, and bees settling in upside down for a cool night's slumber. A magnifying glass, macro lens, or home microscope reveals an exquisite world in miniature: the turquoise eyes and princely crown on the head of a syrphid fly; the antler-like protrusions of a pollen-covered flower beetle who evolved to look like a bumblebee; the punk-rock hairdo of a hickory horned devil caterpillar who will one day morph into a royal walnut moth.

Even some of the animals not new to science will be new to you. Hoping to see javelinas and coyotes outside my mother-in-law's suburban Arizona home one day, I stood still long enough to spot something much rarer to human eyes: a western pygmy blue, one of the smallest butterflies in the world. Easily overlooked because of his diminutive size and low-flying habit, he alighted on the flowers of a desert marigold, the glittering wing pattern coming to life in my viewfinder.

What does it take to find one of the world's smallest butterflies? Sometimes nothing more than stepping outside your back door—as my mother-in-law and I did when we found this western pygmy blue near her home in Scottsdale.

Join the citizen science brigade.

Back home, I've begun to record similar butterfly sightings for a countywide census project. Taken collectively, such data from yards and local natural areas can add to the body of scientific knowledge about wildlife health and habitat. From Minnesota schoolchildren who found deformed frogs in polluted waters to bat detectives who use ultrasonic sensors to identify vocalizations inaudible to human ears, citizen scientists have been instrumental in raising awareness and funding for conservation.

While the efforts help threatened species, they also provide free education and inspiration to amateur naturalists and gardeners. Whether your interest is fungi or slugs or birdcalls, there is a local or national citizen science project—and sometimes even an app—for that. Online keys offered by Bumble Bee Watch make it easy to distinguish among dozens of species, and videos created by the Monarch Larva Monitoring Project train participants to recognize and record butterfly life cycles from egg to adult. FrogWatch USA and FrogWatch in Canada help participants learn frog and toad calls, while the Cornell Lab of Ornithology's YardMap project connects like-minded neighbors online—with the broader goal of connecting habitats across communities.

Recognize the team effort.

When learning who lives in your yard, consider how each animal contributes to the growth and health of her fellow species in unexpected ways. Beetles, the largest group of pollinators, were among the earth's first flower visitors and are important to ancient species with accessible, bowl-shaped blooms like magnolias and Carolina allspice.

Ants carry the seeds of native wildflowers to their young, who nibble on attached lipid-rich fleshy structures called elaiosomes; the adults then haul the still-intact seeds to the community trash pile, where they later germinate into new plants. Snakes, if they're not eaten first, tunnel down into screech owl nests and eat insects that would otherwise parasitize the owlets. The burrows of groundhogs shelter toads who eat slugs, skunks who eat grubs, and other animals who provide free, invaluable assistance to gardeners.

Even in a small yard, you might be surprised by who shows up if you let them. Nature has a way of letting us know when things are finally working—and also when they aren't. Yet we keep fighting her anyway. We mow down life just as it's getting off the ground. We build levees and walls to hold back water, earth, fire, and each other. We add fencing to separate ourselves from the unknown on the other side. In the process we become more disconnected from the species with whom our fates and the fate of the planet are intricately intertwined.[3] It's not difficult to reconnect again, though; we have only to step outside the door, where a world of beauty—and small but significant wonders—awaits.

As the Gulf Coast still struggled to recover seven years after Katrina, the sea began rising in the northeast and destroyed the Staten Island home Loret Setters had loved for twenty-five years. By that time, she was already settled into a new life in Florida. Though she'd escaped the wrath of Hurricane Sandy, her retirement property in the subtropics was subject to flooding as well. At first she resisted, fighting the natural ebb and flow of the rainy seasons so she could walk in the backyard. After recognizing the futility of pumping water from the wetland created by her over-flowing pond—it was like "trying to empty the ocean with a teaspoon," she jokes—Setters solved the problem with a sturdy pair of boots and a slight change of heart. Now she relishes forging a more watery path, one that leaves fewer footprints on the recovering land.

Loret Setters

*retired document processor and
wildlife garden activist*

THE HOME

A one-acre wetland in Saint Cloud, Florida

Little escapes Loret Setters's explorer's-eye view, which leads her to treasures underfoot like this bella moth, whose caterpillars she has also observed feeding on seedpods of rabbitbells. Beautiful in their own right, moths are critical to birds that feed on their larvae; for every North American butterfly species, there are at least fifteen species of moths.

Setters found this pine lily, a threatened species in Florida, growing behind her fence.

Loret Setters walks among the tadpoles, delighting in the bluegills and mosquitofish swimming around her clunky wading boots. She carries her point-and-shoot Nikon to capture lacewing eggs about to hatch on saw palmetto fronds and alligators blinking at her from the edge of her pond. She compares notes with entomologists and horticulturists, each day adding to an ever-growing body of science that seeks to catalog and quantify the remaining biodiversity of our planet.

And it all takes place not in the rainforests of Brazil or Costa Rica but right outside the back door of her mobile home.

"Today I found a new fruit fly," she muses one summer afternoon while recounting other recent wild sightings: species of crickets and spiders she's never seen before, a ribbon snake that eluded her camera, a thoroughwort flower, several kinds of turtles. "I almost mowed over a threatened species last week—a leafless beaked orchid."

Though she'd welcomed the opossums and otters and naturally occurring plants to her Staten Island property before retiring in 2004, Setters had also added her share of harmful species to her gardens. "Please, I was probably the biggest propagator of invasives in the world," she jokes. "And when I moved here, I was like everybody else. Everything was clear-cut, and I just mowed. Everything was grass."

It was modern technology that brought local ecology onto her radar. Enticed onto Twitter by a TV promotion for free movie tickets, she became aware of regional water problems and eventually joined the Florida Native Plant Society. Online conversations with conservationists led to an invitation to join a national team blogging site, where her tagline became "I garden for wildlife—the benefit to my senses is merely a bonus."

Setters's daily postings of new discoveries provide visceral evidence of the life that springs forth when turfgrass is largely abandoned: the many mother spiders whose babies protect the garden from insect attacks, the grasshoppers who might meet their fate in the beaks of birds. She's more excited to find a spider exoskeleton than a monarch butterfly, she says, and her concentrated searches have revealed sights rarely available to others, such as a headless glass lizard still wriggling from his encounter with a hawk.

Her frequent excursions around her property start each morning after she feeds her three dogs. "I just am one with nature for about an hour," she says. "I'm just fascinated by the fact of what happens in this little single acre."

Ask her if she's always been a student of the natural world, and she's unequivocal: "I failed science." Her credentials don't include a knack for gardening either, she insists. "My mother had a green thumb. She could grow anything.... I can't do that."

The lushness surrounding Setters makes that hard to believe—until you come to realize that in this wetland paradise, Mother Nature is the real gardener. Setters leaves unmowed areas each year to see what unexpected treasures will arise. "Once I stopped trying to control what went on out here, the yard really started to come together."

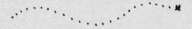

The two-hundred-plus native plant species that accepted her invitation now feed and shelter bald eagles, mockingbirds, turtles, southern leopard frogs, skinks, black racer snakes, milkweed beetles, damselflies, two species of rabbits, and countless other animals. Many plants—wax myrtles that provide berries for bluebirds, passionflower

Green anoles flare their flashy dewlaps to attract females and show territorial dominance. They stalk insects and spiders in the vertical layers —including trees, shrubs, walls, and fences—of moist and shady environments.

Surrounded by pine flatlands and cypress trees, Setters's wetlands home is a haven to green tree frogs, spreadwing damselflies, and other water-loving creatures.

Spanish needles is "my absolutely most favorite flower of all time, and it's probably people's most hated flower of all time," says Setters. "Everybody says, what's it good for?" People complain about its sticky seeds, but those seeds bring cardinals en masse in fall. The leaves are a larval host for emerald moths; the flowers attract syrphid flies, bees, spiders, green anoles, butterflies, and this clouded crimson moth. "It's a playground for wildlife," says Setters.

vines that feed caterpillars of Gulf fritillary butterflies—have been seeded by wind and birds. Even that rare orchid that nearly suffered the fate of death by mower had originally shown up without prompting, made welcome by Setters's unconventional approach to landscaping.

Common species have a special place in this space, too. Cudweed is revered as a larval host of the American lady butterfly, and plantain is nurtured for buckeye butterfly caterpillars. Some plants are even better when they're dead, says Setters, who celebrates her longleaf pine snags for providing nesting habitat for pileated woodpeckers, brown-headed nuthatches, insects, and other tiny creatures. "What do you got against woodpeckers?" she's been known to ask passersby who offer to chop down dead trees for her. Rainy season is now her favorite, partly because storms create nature's ultimate birdhouses. "I hope God is listening to me," she says, "because I could really use a lightning strike."

CHAPTER 3

Is Your Yard Family-Friendly?
Provide Baby Food and Nesting Sites

Birds, bees, and butterflies require special
habitat for their young.

Red-faced and caked in a waxy layer, my newborn nephew looked dangerously oxygen-deprived. But a glance around the room showed that no one else shared my growing alarm. *He's a baby*, the nurse assured me. *That's what babies look like.*

In spite of his alien appearance—or maybe because of it—I loved him instantly, seeing beyond his hairless and helpless exterior to envision the light that would soon turn on in his eyes and the smile that would break across his face.

Such maternal concern and unfettered admiration didn't come as naturally when I was confronted with the messy evidence of a different kind of baby a few years later in a flowerpot on my deck: the half-eaten, tattered leaves rolled together in a layer of gauzy white matter looked a bit like a disease outbreak ready for the sanitation crew. And I'm not alone in my reaction, judging from the guesses audience members make when they see the mystery photos on-screen during my wildlife gardening talks: "It's a spiderweb!" someone invariably shouts out. "It's a mite!" another will say. Then, when

It might look
messy, but this pot
of annual licorice
plant on my deck
turned out to be
the home of butter-
flies in the making.
Caterpillars of
the American lady
species take shelter
inside leaves they
tie together with
silk.

Some of the cater-
pillars became food
for baby birds, but
those who made
it to the adult stage
fed on zinnias on
our deck and native
plants in the garden.

the answer still remains elusive, a brave soul might ask tentatively: "Is it…a fungus?"

I can't remember whether I had any clue what the white fuzz might be when I first came upon it. But closer inspection that evening revealed the source: my flowerpot was a campsite for American lady butterfly babies, who'd fashioned leafy tents where they could hide from predators during the day and come out to feed at night.

As a dietary staple for birds, caterpillars of many butterfly and moth species have developed elaborate ways to protect themselves from winged predators. Some disguises are much harder for humans to spot, but the chosen camouflage of American lady babies can backfire in the face of our appearance-obsessed culture, as can the lifestyles of countless other common insects. Often through a fear of the unknown, exacerbated by marketing ploys of pesticide manufacturers, even gardeners trying to create more welcoming spaces for wildlife take on perceived messes and invasions with disproportionate resolve. "I used a pesticide in my butterfly garden after finding a lot of bugs on my milkweed plant," a blog reader emailed me one summer. "Took a picture and posted it on Facebook and learned that this bug is a milkweed bug. Did I destroy my butterfly garden?"

The level of damage would depend on the chemical sprayed, but it's possible that generations of other species were harmed in the gardener's zeal to kill a tiny creature that, like the vast majority of insects, are harmless and lead fascinating lives in their own right. Though not as glamorous as the butterflies she'd hoped to attract, milkweed bugs lay eggs on their namesake plant and feed primarily on its seeds their whole lives; some also migrate up and down the continent to catch the seed heads post-bloom. Ironically, the esteem in

Antipathy toward certain species can have dire consequences even for the ones a gardener is trying to save. Refraining from spraying any denizens of the milkweed patch, including milkweed bugs and milkweed beetles, will keep the plants healthy for monarchs and others as well.

Labeled "pests" by at least one monarch conservation organization because of their appetite for milkweed, slugs are just as important to the ecology of a garden as monarchs are. Though some gardeners kill them with beer, diatomaceous earth, and other products, these animals break down organic material and serve as food for toads, birds, turtles, and beetles. If you leave fallen leaves on the ground and plant a range of species that welcome both slugs and their predators, you won't even notice the nibbling.

which people hold these interesting animals seems inversely related to opinions about their host plant: those who view milkweed as a lawn and crop invader consider milkweed bugs beneficial because their voracious seed-eating limits the plants' spread; those who grow milkweed solely for butterflies tend to regard other visitors as intruders.

While saddened by the unnecessary loss of life, I didn't blame my well-intentioned fellow gardener for being confused. She is part of a national epidemic in which homeowners and landscapers apply chemicals indiscriminately. And that seems to be how manufacturers prefer it. Promising gorgeous roses in magical, happy flower kingdoms, their ads encourage us to spray first and think later, or, preferably, not think much at all about the havoc we're wreaking.

Ending the assault on tiny wild families

Nowhere was that attitude more apparent than during the start of National Pollinator Week in 2013. Normally a time to celebrate the bees, butterflies, beetles, bats, hummingbirds, and other creatures whose hard work is central to the food supply of people and animals across the planet, the event turned into a time of mourning for bee advocates. Two days before the official launch, an unprecedented disaster unfolded in the parking lot of a suburban Portland shopping center. In a painful illustration of why we need special weeks devoted to imperiled species, bees rained down from trees by the thousands. By the time shoppers noticed, many were dead. Others writhed on the ground or flew frantically among the trees.

"I'd never seen anything like that before," says Rich Hatfield, a conservation biologist at the Xerces Society for Invertebrate Conservation who was called to investigate. "You literally couldn't walk anywhere without hearing the crunch of carcasses under your feet."

The official estimated body count reached at least fifty thousand, but the number may have been greater. Cause of death: an insecticide sprayed on flowering linden trees to kill aphids. Reason for spraying: the aphids were secreting honeydew, a sticky but easily washed-off substance on shoppers' cars. "Who knows how many animals died that day for literally no reason?" asks Hatfield. "It was maddening to me, how something like that could happen."

Sacrificed for the sake of appearances, the bees were collateral damage of our selective compassion, their plight illustrating a cultural blindness to the cascade effects of human antipathy toward any single species. Since then, the now infamous crime against nature has been repeated—Oregon saw at least nine similar incidents over

As they forage on flower after flower, female bees pick up many pollen grains on their bodies. They push them to tufts of hair on their legs or abdomen called scopa, carrying them back to the nest for their offspring. If they happen to visit plants pretreated with systemic insecticides, mother bees risk ingesting potentially toxic nectar and transferring contaminated pollen to their young.

the following two years, and it's likely happening all over the country, says Hatfield.

It's uncertain whether the mass die-offs were a result of the insecticide exclusively or of its use on a particular species; linden trees contain a sugar bumblebees can't break down, so consumption of large quantities may cause the insects to appear temporarily drunk and fall to the ground. But linden nectar alone isn't known to kill the bees, "who get up and fly around, and they're fine," says Hatfield. The same can't be said for neonicotinoids, the class of systemic pesticides implicated in the incidents.

When mixed into soil, sprayed onto leaves, and coated on seeds, these substances turn nature on itself, entering a plant's vascular system and conscripting every part of it, including pollen and nectar, into a chemical weapon. "What systemic insecticides are doing," says entomologist Vera Krischik, an associate professor at the University of Minnesota, "is they're breaking up 146 million years of coevolution."

In addition to harming birds directly, pesticides destroy their food supply. Because we've never used chemicals of any kind, this Carolina wren and his mate were able to feed their babies a rich banquet of beetle larvae, moths, caterpillars, spiders, and other arthropods.

While bees are the most well-known pollinators, she explains, other insects have an ancient relationship with flowers, which first appeared on the geologic scene following the end of the Jurassic period. Even if they do not effectively transfer pollen from one flower to another, many species have evolved to sip nectar and eat pollen as a source of protein.

In study after study, Krischik and others have demonstrated the adverse effects of neonicotinoids on a diverse range of animals, including bumblebees, honeybees, ladybugs, green lacewings, and caterpillars of monarch and painted lady butterflies. In some cases, as with the butterfly larvae, the animals died outright following ingestion of treated leaves. In others, as with bumblebees, they experienced sublethal effects from contaminated pollen and nectar—reduced foraging ability, smaller nesting growth, and declines in queen production.[1]

Though neonicotinoids are often touted as safer for birds, a songbird can die after ingesting corn kernels coated with imidacloprid, the most widely used neonicotinoid. Downstream effects are just as injurious when the chemicals diminish insect populations that birds eat. A study in the Netherlands found an alarming average 3.5 percent annual decline in bird populations in areas with higher surface-water concentrations of imidacloprid; the researchers suggested lack of food as a probable cause, along with possible poisonings by ingestion of seeds or insects contaminated by the pesticide.[2]

The toxicity of neonicotinoids to wildlife is so well documented that bottled sprays contain EPA-mandated warnings of the chemicals' high toxicity to bees, aquatic invertebrates, and fish. The labels issue a litany of instructions that would be comical if they weren't so sad: Do not apply when rain is predicted. Do not apply while bees are foraging or when plants are flowering. Do not apply until all flower petals have fallen off. To reduce bee kills, minimize drift onto beehives or "off-site pollinator attractive habitat"—in other words, your neighbor's wildflower garden.

As dire as the warnings sound, they still sidestep the most insidious aspect of systemic insecticides: that regardless of how you apply them, the chemicals will be absorbed into all plant parts and delivered back to visiting insects later—a fact not lost on scientists and bee advocates, who are pressuring retailers to stop selling pretreated nursery stock to unsuspecting gardeners. Although some companies have responded, their actions often carry a cynical twist, embodied in plant tags that began appearing in pots of forsythia, hollies, and other common garden stock sold at Home Depot stores in the spring of 2015. Far from the expected warning about potential toxicity to bees, the language of the new consumer labels instead focused on insects most people have been taught to hate: "This plant is protected from problematic aphids/white flies/beetles/mealy bugs and other unwanted pests by neonicotinoids," read the front, with the back side referring consumers to a web address that included the words "Eco Options" and "healthy home." By casting the chemicals as protective safeguards against six-legged trespassers, the new plant labels' linguistic trickery promulgated the arbitrary notion that some animals are better than others, ignoring the importance of nearly all insects in the ecosystem—as nutrient recyclers, predators, food sources, and pollinators.

The negative fallout was swift, and less than a year later, the retailer pledged to phase out plants pretreated with neonicotinoids altogether by the end of 2018, joining a growing list of nurseries and suppliers looking for alternatives. Legislators are taking notice; in 2015 Ontario became the first jurisdiction in North America to commit to reduction of acreage planted in neonicotinoid-coated corn and soybean seeds; the next year, Maryland became the first US state to pass a law that will remove general homeowner access to the pesticides. More than twenty cities have voted to eliminate or curtail their use.

It's a start, but as long as bottles of toxic chemicals of many kinds still line retail shelves and pervade our landscapes, these actions alone are not nearly enough. Defenders of neonicotinoids argue that limits on their use will increase the use of harsher pesticides that kill on contact. They may be right. But everyone has a choice, and the most humane option for gardeners is not to buy any of them at all.

Beetles are both pollinators and predators, providing natural insect control. As adults, soldier beetles feast on the possumhaw viburnum and goldenrod flowers in our garden, but at the larval stage, they eat aphids, caterpillars, and other soft-bodied insects.

The most well-known finicky invertebrates, monarch caterpillars, subsist exclusively on milkweed plants. They're in solid company: 90 percent of herbivorous insects are specialists, able to digest only the plants with which they coevolved.

Planting for monarchs also helps bees and many other creatures who depend on milkweed nectar or foliage.

Creating habitat for the forgotten young

Some pesticides, designed to kill plants, hurt wild families indirectly by eliminating their food. The most widely used has been implicated as a significant factor in the decline of monarchs. Applied in fields of genetically modified soy and corn bred to withstand the herbicide, glyphosate—the active ingredient in Roundup—decimates milkweeds that host monarch caterpillars and nectar plants that sustain adult butterflies on their long migrations.

Hope has come in the form of strong public response to the monarch's plight, as gardeners scramble to replace lost habitat for this rock star of invertebrates. Throughout the warm months, my Twitter feed is filled with updates showing the success of these endeavors: A monarch just landed on someone's milkweed in Texas! A caterpillar in California is ready to pupate! Two chrysalises are busting open under chard leaves in Ohio! And somewhere in Minnesota, an egg has been laid! I'm far from immune to monarch madness myself; it's hard not to become obsessed once you learn how shortsighted our own species has been in accelerating the loss of the iconic butterfly's only food supply.

Though the growing awareness is heartening, the singular focus on one animal has also been troubling to scientists trying to save so many others. Following a $3.2 million commitment by the US Fish and Wildlife Service to plant milkweed, University of Hawaii entomologist Daniel Rubinoff lamented in a February 2015 *Washington Post* op-ed that public and private funds devoted to the cause represented "money lost to the conservation of the unsung multitudes of rare insects that will never get their day in the sun." [3]

Fortunately, monarch habitat is beneficial to a broad range of species. But many lesser-known animals seeking other kinds of increasingly scarce food and shelter desperately need our attention, too. Though monarch populations in the eastern United States have dropped precipitously, the species isn't globally rare, unlike the Kern primrose sphinx moth or the spruce-fir moss spider, animals Rubinoff says are surviving on "postage stamps of remaining habitat."

Up to a third of North American bumblebee species are at risk of the same fate, and one, the Franklin's bumblebee, hasn't been seen since 2006 and may be extinct. Yet the habitat needs of these animals are often obscured by another celebrity insect whose popularity rivals that of the monarch: the honeybee, an import first introduced by European settlers. Despite the tendency to associate buzzing honeybee hives with bee conservation, there's little correlation between the two. "Keeping honeybees to save pollinators or to save bees," notes Hatfield, "is very similar to keeping chickens to save birds."

Important pollinators in their own right, the four thousand native bee species in the United States and Canada don't live in hives, don't make honey, and can't be replenished by ordering up a starter kit online. As York University assistant professor Sheila Colla has noted on the blog *Liber Ero*, "Once they are gone, they are gone forever." The consequences of their disappearance would be devastating, since many wild animals depend on the fruit and seeds of plants they pollinate. Our own food supply is also at risk: bumblebees are more effective than honeybees in pollinating many of our favorite crops, including tomatoes, potatoes, and blueberries.[4]

While bumblebees live in small colonies, most native bee species are solitary; about 70 percent nest underground, and the rest find cavities in twigs, logs, and other woody material. With no prefab home base, they rely on us to foster and protect these habitats. And

Hives aren't made by native bees (a common misconception), most of whom nest underground. The crafters of this artistic home were bald-faced hornets, native wasps often characterized as aggressive despite their tendency to leave everyone but fellow insects—and humans who come too close to the nest—alone. Come winter, birds and other animals poke at the vacant hive for insect squatters.

that means resisting the temptation to add an artificial honeybee hive where it's not needed. The benefits of honeybee keeping come with trade-offs for other bees. Disease transmission to wild bee populations has been a major concern, as has competition for limited resources. "When you have a hive in your backyard, you're introducing fifty thousand mouths to feed," Hatfield says, "and that [requires] somewhere between a half acre and an acre of habitat to support them."

Other well-intentioned efforts to help animals in our backyards can have negative consequences for wildlife. Though Americans spend billions of dollars to hang feeders filled with seeds and berries, such handouts are largely useless to growing avian families. The nestlings of 96 percent of North American terrestrial bird species survive on spiders and insects, mostly caterpillars, who are themselves babies with specialized habitat needs. While their milkweed-only diet has made monarch caterpillars the poster children for specialized relationships with plants, most other herbivorous insects—a surprising 90 percent—are also discriminating foodies who can digest only the vegetation they've evolved alongside.[5]

That's a problem for those trying to eke out an existence in suburban yards, where 80 percent of the plants are nonnative and the typical lot has only 10 percent of the tree biomass of a natural woodlot, according to research by University of Delaware entomologist and ecologist Doug Tallamy, author of *Bringing Nature Home: How You Can Sustain Wildlife with Native Plants*. Fewer digestible leaves for insects, of course, means fewer insects—one of his studies found that native species support thirty-five times more caterpillar biomass than do nonnative plants. Without these tiny animals, larger ones, from toads to bats, go hungry; even mammals like foxes and bears satisfy

The caterpillar effect: black cherry trees in entomologist Doug Tallamy's yard host hundreds of species of caterpillars. Many become baby food for the young of birds like this prothonotary warbler. Most bird parents need thousands of caterpillars to raise a single brood to the fledgling stage.

a quarter of their nutrition needs by eating insects. And it doesn't take just a few minifauna to sustain other animals; at less than half an ounce, tiny chickadee parents need up to nine thousand caterpillars to raise a single brood to the fledgling stage.

To help creatures across the food web, consider the following tips for creating and protecting habitat for young animals in your yard.

Plant baby food.

Rather than putting out seed, look at plants in your garden as baby bird feeders, Tallamy advises. If you have the space, cater to caterpillar gourmands by adding oaks, black cherries, and willows, which feed hundreds of species of butterflies and moths at the larval stage. Plant asters, goldenrods, and other native perennials that do double duty, with leaves that nourish caterpillars and flowers that feed adult pollinators.[6]

They both enjoy the nectar of joe-pye weed as adults, but these butterflies (top) previously had different diets. The caterpillars of great spangled fritillary need violets, while those of the more diminutive pearl crescent consume asters. The variegated fritillary caterpillar (bottom) has a broader palate but also includes violets in her diet. Conveniently, mothers lay eggs near the plants in late summer so larvae can begin eating in spring.

The greater the plant diversity in your garden, the more animals you'll have at the buffet. Though many native bees provision nests with pollen and nectar from a range of flowers, a number are floral specialists, relying on pollen of certain plant lineages; *Andrena violae*, a kind of mining bee, prefers violets, while *Lasioglossum oenotherae*, a sweat bee, gathers pollen from evening primroses.[7]

Don't mow down the teenagers.

Lack of plant diversity isn't the only challenge for new generations in the wild. The cultivation practices required to maintain a manicured green lawn disrupt the life cycles of grasshoppers and other ground dwellers. Fritillary butterflies don't stand a chance against power machinery because they overwinter as larvae near ground-hugging violets, which are their host plants. "So they survive the winter under the snow, and then they crawl up on those violets just as they're poking above our grass, and we come along, and we murder them all with our mowers," says Tallamy. "So that's it for your fritillaries."

Take a pass on turfgrass, using it only for walkways or small seating or play areas. In places where you still want low-growing plants, mix native wildflowers with indigenous grasses and groundcovers that nurture life above- and belowground.

Support the homebuilding industry.

Leaves aren't just food for herbivorous insects; they're also construction material. While we cut down trees to build our own shelter from the storms, industrious leafcutter bees are excising round holes from foliage and flower petals to line tiny nests in logs, old beetle burrows, or rock crevices. Like artists sculpting a bowl on a pottery wheel, mothers craft chewed-up plant material into cup shapes before filling them with pollen and nectar and laying their eggs.

The process can take up to three hours for one nest cell, says Olivia Messinger Carril, whose admiration for native mother bees inspired her dedication to them in the book she coauthored with Joseph Wilson, *The Bees in Your Backyard: A Guide to North America's Bees*. Unlike honeybees, they die after ensuring a safe home for their young. "They never get the pleasure that I do of seeing their babies," says Carril, a mother of two. "So everything they do is devoted to ensuring their little babies are as well off as they can possibly be because Mom's going to be gone—the building of the perfect nest and getting just the right pollen."

The plants have evolved to withstand the nibbling; fossil evidence indicates that leafcutter bees have been busy making hole-punch shapes for more than thirty million years. As gardeners, we can evolve to withstand a little nibbling, too, learning to celebrate the holes in our leaves as a sign that our garden is nurturing wild families of species large and small.

Replace poisons with natural insect control.

Instead of using pesticides that kill animals at every life stage, encourage the animals themselves to provide natural insect control. Dragonflies are voracious consumers of mosquitoes, eating up to three hundred a day, while a single bat can devour thousands of insects each night. Syrphid flies pollinate flowers as adults but snack on thrips, scales, mealybugs, spider mites, and as many as fifty aphids daily while in the larval stage. Wasps can be both predators and parasitoids; some collect caterpillars and stinkbugs for their larvae,

A leafcutter bee excises pieces of fireweed foliage (above), which she will use to line her nest in a Wisconsin backyard. The bees lay eggs in logs, rocks, and even seemingly unlikely cavities such as this unused pipe in New Brunswick (right).

Dragonflies perch atop left-over flower stalks to search for prey and eating up to three hundred mosquitoes a day (top). By letting these volunteer bonesets proliferate on my property, I put out the welcome mat for beautiful blue-winged wasps (left), who kill Japanese beetle grubs by laying their eggs in them. An assassin bug nymph, a voracious predator, joins the party (bottom).

THE HUMANE GARDENER

while others lay their eggs in insects like tomato hornworms, who slowly die as the larvae grow into adults.

Welcome these animals to the garden by planting natives, which attract a greater diversity of species.[8] Though I didn't know it at the time, the boneset that volunteered on my property introduced an unexpected natural control; blue-winged wasps, who are especially fond of the plant's late summer blooms, began visiting them in droves, often pausing to hover above the nearby grass and lay their eggs in Japanese beetle grubs just below the surface.

Protect hidden nurseries.

A bare patch of dirt, a leftover perennial stalk, a tree cavity: it's not so much to ask for. Yet these simple habitats for native bee nests are often lacking in the typical yard. Rather than adding a honeybee hive, think of yourself as a beekeeper for all the wild species visiting your garden. Keep sunny, unmulched areas where ground-nesting mothers can tunnel. Leave pithy stalks for wood nesters, pruning some at the top to create access for species that don't excavate their own holes. Depending on where you live, bee nesting sites could include hollow stems of goldenrod, roses, raspberry, sumac, sagebrush, buckwheat, elderberry, false willow, and blackberry.

Bumblebees are opportunistic nesters, finding cozy spots in old bird nests, hollow logs, dead trees, rocks, compost piles, vacant bird-houses, and abandoned mouse and squirrel burrows. (Avoid roden-ticides; cruel products in their own right, they also eliminate these potential homes for pollinators.) Keep leaves in place under trees and shrubs, where they'll shelter butterfly pupae and queen bumblebees resting up to start new families in the spring. Buried in the rich soil

Beneath coral honeysuckle vines and other host plants, the caterpillars of beautiful snowberry clearwing moths (left)—often likened to tiny hummingbirds—overwinter as pupae. Under sumacs and wax myrtles are the young of red-banded hairstreak butterflies (below), whose mothers lay their eggs on the fallen leaves.

Butterflies gather on fruit, carrion, and muddy areas—including driveways—to collect moisture and nutrients, including minerals thought to enhance reproduction. After wastefully watering the driveway to help visiting red-spotted purples (right), we created a more sustainable option: puddling dishes filled with sand and topped with a thin layer of soil, pebbles, and a bit of water (top). Within minutes a common buckeye came for a long sip.

Native host plants for the American lady butterfly include these Parlin's pussytoes and other plants in the *Antennaria* genus. Cudweed and pearly everlasting also feed the caterpillars of this species.

are also fireflies in the making; unlike ground-nesting bees, mother fireflies need leaf litter and humidity for their larvae, who feast there on snails, slugs, and insects. "It's our propensity to clean up and make sure there's nothing on the ground," says Tallamy, "but bare soil is instant death to these guys."

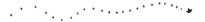

Back on my deck, the mother of my American lady butterfly caterpillars had chosen a pot of licorice plants, an annual native to southern Africa, for her nursery, sending me to the garden center for more to ensure no one ran out of food. Seeking a more permanent host for the next generation in my garden, I later planted two of their preferred native groundcovers, plainleaf pussytoes and Parlin's pussytoes. Less than two weeks later, caterpillars were already taking shelter in the plants. Their fuzzy tents taught me to see "messes" all over the garden much differently: the tent caterpillars on the cherry trees and the sawfly larvae on the dogwoods may look unkempt to human eyes, but they are somebody's babies—and may even feed somebody else's, as bluebirds and chickadees and Carolina wrens swoop in to find soft meals to carry back to their growing families.

As gardeners and stewards of the earth, we should have the courage and humility to add habitat that welcomes the babies of all species, as Charlotte Adelman has done in her own backyard and in the larger sanctuary she created in the center of a busy Illinois suburb. Refusing to accept the lot she was handed when she bought her house, Adelman filled it not just with pretty flowers but also host plants for hundreds of species, creating the world she wanted to live in—one that embraces our fellow travelers through this life: wings, stings, messy nests, and all.

THE HUMANE
GARDENER

Charlotte Adelman

retired lawyer and conservationist

THE HOME

*A backyard woodland and two-acre prairie
in urban Wilmette, Illinois*

The two-acre prairie that Charlotte Adelman has created in a community park is just one project among many she's taken on in the name of the environment. The author of three books on native plants and prairies, she also spent years fighting for passage of ordinances regulating pesticides and leaf blowers.

It's difficult to take a quiet, private tour of Charlotte Adelman's garden in the Chicago suburbs. The lush oasis is simply too popular with local party animals—the woodpecker who bangs away while Adelman points out the squirrel houses in the cottonwood trees, the chattering songbird whose tune overtakes her narrative about the successional white blooms of Washington hawthorns, gray dogwoods, black locusts, elderberries, and cow parsnips gracing the shady Eden.

Adelman pauses to take note of the persistent interruptions. "There's that chickadee again. They just love these feeders."

"I want to encourage them," she says of her many animal visitors. "People don't like this animal or that animal—'they're ugly,' 'they're scary,' or whatever. I love them all. They have a right, in my view, anyway, to prosper."

As do the plants that feed and shelter them. Adelman has so many in her yard that she sometimes has to consult the book she cowrote with her husband, Bernard Schwartz, *The Midwestern Native Garden: Native Alternatives to Nonnative Flowers and Plants*, to remember their names. From the seven oak trees that feed the caterpillars of hundreds of butterfly and moth species to the thriving jewelweed patch that nourishes hummingbirds, each plant has a purpose—often many purposes—beyond mere decoration. "This is a cup plant," Adelman says. "The leaves form cups, and the water stays, and the birds will drink from it and such. And if you're in a country area, frogs will be in there.... They get yellow flowers; butterflies love them, and the birds love the seeds."

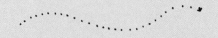

Blooming purple coneflower is a magnet for bees and butterflies like this eastern tiger swallowtail. In late summer, goldfinches—described by the Cornell Lab of Ornithology as "among the strictest vegetarians in the bird world"—descend on the seed heads. When Adelman witnessed this special plant-animal relationship in a neighbor's garden, she vowed to transform her own.

Adelman used to fill her lot with hostas and other exotic species, until one day on a walk through the neighborhood she spotted a bright yellow goldfinch feasting on the seed head of a purple coneflower. "It just sort of made me realize these birds were relying on native plants, really, for food," she says. It was a dramatic contrast to her garden of Asian daylilies, which drew virtually no wildlife. "They were just sitting there," she says of the species she now calls "plastic plants." "They don't attract any kind of pollinator; they don't host any butterflies."

The epiphany launched a one-woman movement that eventually resulted in a community prairie, carved out of a sea of turfgrass a few blocks away. On a quick drive to the site, Adelman laments the municipal plantings lining the streets—gingko trees that support the needs of few (if any) animal species, lilacs added only for the sake of "three days of white flowers," she says. "You just look at it, and you think: Why?"

This urbanized area sixteen miles north of Chicago is rife with parks, bike trails, ice rinks, tennis courts, theaters, and swimming pools—a wealth of human habitat that earned Wilmette a spot on a list of top places in the country to raise a family. But as in most suburbs, considerably fewer amenities exist for other species in need of places to raise young. At two acres, Adelman's dazzling wildflower patch, installed near a busy village intersection, occupies a fraction of the twenty-two million acres of prairie that once blanketed the state. It's enough to support what mowed-down landscapes in the area can't, though. Beneath the low roar of thousands of cars and trucks zooming by each day, something else is abuzz if you stop long enough to listen: the quieter undercurrent of many more species making a life here.

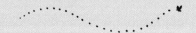

A retired attorney whose caseload once included a fight against sexist *Chicago Tribune* want-ad listings, Adelman doesn't hesitate to take on injustice when she sees it. When pesticide warning signs went up on the lawn of a local library where children were reading, "it just seemed wrong to me," she says. She worked for years to persuade the village board to stop using such chemicals in public spaces.

Gas-powered leaf blowers were another target: dismayed by their noise and pollution, Adelman successfully fought for a ban on their use in late spring and summer.

With the blessing and assistance of the park district, she and a local Boy Scout began creating the prairie in 2010 with ten pounds of seed Adelman purchased from a native plant seller. A few years later, a spectacular range of color lights up the former detention basin originally created to slow storm runoff. While gardeners cultivate vegetables in the community plots on the other side of the park, butterflies search for places to lay their eggs in the prairie—host plants chosen specifically for caterpillars who can digest only leaves they coevolved with. As the sounds of children splashing in a village pool mingle with birdsong and traffic, red-winged blackbird parents perch atop milkweed, protecting their nests in the middle of the gentle valley. "To me that's exciting," says Adelman. "Though it is a common bird, nonetheless it's important that something can actually live in here and reproduce."

Adelman watches over her prairie with much the same vigilance as the blackbirds, weeding out invaders like Queen Anne's lace that threaten animal habitat. When she thinks she has spotted destructive dame's rocket, she's delighted to realize she's wrong. "You know what this is? It's one of my alternatives!" she says, referring to her book's

A red-winged blackbird guards
a nest in the prairie.

In Adelman's garden (below), blue false indigo hosts caterpillars of some butterfly species, including the wild indigo duskywing and the cloudless sulphur, while golden alexander feeds black swallowtail butterflies at the larval stage.

Cleopatra, a former stray rescued by Adelman and her husband, enjoys traversing the miniwoodland, where queen of the prairie blooms light up the path in early summer.

extensive guide to native substitutes for commonly planted nonnative species. "A prairie phlox. When there are a lot of them, it's gorgeous."

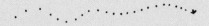

Implicit in Adelman's personal gardening and public activism is a defiance of the cultural standards that have made so many landscapes inhospitable to all but our own species. Many of the plants in her garden are proxies for those lost to the apathy of a culture in love with chain saws. One neighbor for years protected his beloved black walnut, a tree with leaves that host luna and regal moths, nuts that feed squirrels and birds, and a canopy that provides roosting sites for owls. When the man died in his nineties, the new homeowners "cut it down immediately—for no reason. They didn't expand their house or anything," says Adelman. "So I decided to put one in."

Black walnuts have an undeserved reputation as plant killers; their roots leach chemicals that prove unwelcoming to some garden species. But as Adelman's backyard proves, walnuts have grown in concert with native species for millennia. From the hazelnut to the fringe tree, the gray dogwoods to the black cherries, the blue false indigo to the forked aster to the diminutive white avens, the garden flourishes at every layer of the canopy. In spite of the lack of habitat in surrounding yards, monarchs even manage to find the abundant milkweed in the shadow of a redbud in the front yard.

Back at the prairie, they find even more diversity: five kinds of milkweed that feed their larvae and liatris flowers that satisfy their own nectaring needs. Bees, skippers, dragonflies, and red admiral butterflies join them, floating over all the other colors and textures of the summer palette: the fuzzy pink of joe-pye weed, the smiling

A monarch comes in for a landing on one
of the prairie's five species of milkweed.

Blue vervain is among
the many prairie plants providing foliage for cater-
pillars and nectar and pollen
for adult butterflies and
bees. Native Turk's-cap lily
could easily hold its own
in a beauty contest with
exotic daylilies.

faces of yellow native sunflowers, the ethereal blue vervain flowers, the button-topped purple prairie clover, the popping orange Turk's-cap lilies, the delicate white dogbane flowers belying their sturdy stalks. Bare patches of ground provide nesting sites for native bees, and goldfinches and other birds descend on seed heads in late summer and fall. Native grasses give cover to rabbits and robins, food to skipper larvae, and shelter for the prairie's flashy nightlife.

By twilight, when many of the animals retreat into dense vegetation, fireflies will emerge over the basin—so many that on one warm evening Adelman and her husband pull themselves out of bed to witness a spectacle made possible only by the lack of pesticides, fertilizers, and disturbance, a display she likens to thousands of blinking Christmas lights. It's not a phenomenon that would occur in the denuded environment just outside the prairie, where an afternoon tour ends when a man with a gas-powered trimmer walks around listlessly aiming at vegetation daring to sprout in cracks in the sidewalk. It's too loud for humans to talk anymore now. But the blackbirds guarding their nests and the butterflies laying their eggs just inside the prairie borders pay him no mind. They know where they're wanted, even if this is life on the edge.

CHAPTER 4

Safety Zones: Create Sanctuary in a Treacherous World

––––––––––

*Wild animals face hidden hazards in our
yards and gardens.*

The tiny eastern box turtle had already evaded many predators: foxes, skunks, raccoons, opossums, and crows who wouldn't mind having a few eggs or a soft-shelled baby for breakfast. Yet here at the edge of our yard, in a patch of overgrown grasses, the young reptile was confronting an opponent his millions of years of evolution had not prepared him for: a weed-whacker.

Once they reach maturity, box turtles may roam their small territories for fifty years on average, with some living much longer. Their longevity is part of their survival strategy, intended to ensure they can replace themselves at least once.

For most of their time on the planet, this worked. Turtles could move freely beneath trees and through clearings, eating berries, leaves, slugs, worms, insects, and other denizens of forests, meadows, and ponds. Once mature, they still had to worry about being eaten themselves, but only by other hungry animals.

It's taken just decades for this wonder of nature to spiral into decline. Protective turtle shells, even adult ones, are no match for

It would be a few more years before the shell of this young box turtle (above) hardened, but he'd already managed to elude foxes, raccoons, opossums, and other predators in our yard. Even the solid shells of older turtles can't protect them from man-made hazards. Hit by a lawn mower in Massachusetts, this adult turtle (left) spent months at the Cape Wildlife Center, where animal caretakers repaired the damage to his shell.

power equipment in farm fields and gardens, cars zooming down roads that transect dwindling habitat, and an exploitive pet trade that captures the animals from the wild. Like so many other species, turtles have not had time to evolve any defense mechanisms against the excesses of human civilization.

Our young turtle was fine because we'd inspected the area before trimming back the invasive grasses from the edge of a new meadow. But years before, not long after we moved into our home, an adult turtle suffered a different fate, succumbing to the blades of our old industrial-sized mower. We've since seen other turtles, but I'll spend the rest of my life trying to make it up to that one. In an era of ever-increasing development, the untimely death of just a few adults could propel a local population to eventual extinction.[1] Habitat fragmentation exacerbates the fragility of the balance, marooning animals into obsolescence. We don't have any more time or turtles to spare.

Picking up the pieces

Wildlife rescuers and rehabilitators know what's at stake more viscerally than most of us, as they struggle to put back together broken shells, damaged wings, and punctured intestines of creatures caught up in our machines and our trash. While we often treat our houses and yards as transactional spaces to be perpetually bought and sold, these animals are trying to make a permanent life in the only home they've ever known. Creatures of habit, they tend to follow the same patterns in limited territories year after year, sometimes for generations.

In the process, they encounter constantly shifting environments their evolution has not prepared them for. In just a single season, emergency responses by Maryland state biologists included a range of mishaps that befall animals all too frequently across the continent: a deer entangled in soccer netting, a red-tailed hawk stuck in a volleyball net, a bear with his head jammed in a metal milk jug, a fox caught in twine, and an osprey hooked by a discarded fishing lure.

"It's a tough world out there for urban animals," says Paula Goldberg, the executive director of City Wildlife, a Washington, DC, nonprofit that regularly treats pigeons with string wrapped in their toes, squirrels orphaned when trees are removed, and birds caught in netting. "A home lawn and garden is not a benign place for them."

One of the organization's most unusual patients was an American toad, considered a species of greatest conservation need in the District. From his inch-and-a-half-long frame dangled a hind leg, nearly sliced off in an encounter with a blade many times his size. Delivered for treatment by a man who'd inadvertently run over him with a push mower, the toad received antibiotics applied directly to his permeable skin from an eyedropper.

In spite of his ordeal, he was one of the few animals lucky to be found by someone who cared enough to help him. If we all move a little more thoughtfully through the landscape and watch out for the following dangers, we can minimize harm to many more species just trying to make a life in our yards.

Know before you mow.

To help amphibians and other small animals leap out of the path of danger, do a walkabout to check for animals before firing up the power equipment. Mow from the inside out, starting at the center of your lawn to give animals time to move to the periphery and avoid

Reaching a length of two to four inches as adults, young American toads can be less than a centimeter when fully metamorphosed— and can easily be injured by lawn mowers.

Mowing and weeding can disturb baby rabbits, who are often left in dense vegetation while their mother forages nearby. To determine if she's still caring for them, place twine over the brush in a crisscross pattern. If the twine is askew in the morning, she has likely come back.

An animal rescuer frees a snake from netting a gardener had placed on a flowerbed in Maryland (below), while in California, a gopher snake caught in the same predicament ended up in treatment at the Fund for Animals Wildlife Center (left).

being trapped in the center. If you have an island of bushes or habitat, let the mower run nearby for a few minutes to encourage frogs and toads to seek temporary refuge elsewhere. Be on the lookout for rabbit nests, which are often camouflaged among groundcovers and tall grasses.

Avoid un-safety nets.

Soccer and volleyball nets are nearly invisible at night to deer and birds, who may panic and die before anyone realizes their plight. Snakes are particularly vulnerable to garden netting. "They're stuck, so they can be preyed upon and harassed by other animals," says Goldberg. "They'll struggle, and sometimes they'll get a laceration where the netting rubbed into their skin."

To prevent such unnecessary suffering, put recreational netting and hammocks away when not in use, and choose more humane deterrents to protect plants. (See Chapter 5 for alternatives to garden netting.) Remove fallen fences, wires, and twine, which can become entangled in the legs of foxes and other animals.

Take down deadly decor.

Fake cobwebs do much more than scare young trick-or-treaters on Halloween; a western screech owl in Marin, California, and a downy woodpecker in Washington, DC, are just two animals who made headlines after getting caught in the sticky substance. Other outdoor adornments, from Christmas lights to metal garden accents, can entangle wildlife and should be monitored frequently if used.

Reduce reflection.

Rather than adding hazardous ornaments to the landscape, channel your decorating skills into preventing window strikes, which kill hundreds of millions of birds each year. To reduce the chances of a bird mistaking a reflection for an extension of his habitat, use streamers, or ribbons, opaque decals, mesh screens, reflective tape, pie plates, and other items that help break the mirage.

Lights out.

Glaring outdoor lamps disrupt the natural cycles of fireflies and other creatures of the night. Giant silk moths, who don't eat as adults, are particularly vulnerable to light pollution, exhausting themselves in the glare. "Once the moth is attracted to the light, it doesn't leave," says entomologist Doug Tallamy. "So it's not out laying its eggs, the males are not finding the females. Any bats that remain pick them off at the light." Prevent harm by using motion lights that will illuminate your path only when necessary.

Polyphemus and other giant silk moths live only a few days and lack mouth parts to eat, making them even more vulnerable to exhaustion from circling lights at night.

FrogLogs help animals escape from swimming pools by providing an angled exit ramp.

Shut your death traps.

Sunken wells around basement windows are like hidden cliff edges for unsuspecting skunks, snakes, toads, salamanders, mice, rabbits, and even fawns. Keep animals from falling by installing a window well cover, available for a few dollars at hardware stores. For those already trapped, angle a board as an exit ramp. A fallen skunk won't be able to climb well, but you can rescue her by lowering a kitchen garbage can tipped on its side and containing a hunk of cheese; then gently lift the can once the skunk has entered it to collect her reward, place it on the ground facing away from you, and wait for her to leave.

Station lifeguards.

The vertical walls of man-made bodies of water are also deadly to animals. Install a FrogLog or Critter Skimmer to provide angled escape routes for toads, mice, spiders, and other small creatures who fall into swimming pools. Add sloping sides in artificial ponds to create accessible getaways. If you build a pond with a liner in colder regions, dig deeper than two feet to protect aquatic frogs from freezing to death at the bottom during the winter.

Despite efforts to save him, a barn owl whose wing was injured after being caught in a fence in California died during treatment at a wildlife rehabilitation center.

Don't fence them in.

Fences can separate mothers from young and ensnare birds, coyotes, foxes, turtles, and other species. They put rabbits in harm's way by limiting natural escape routes from predators. Spiked black metal fences are the most problematic, frequently impaling deer and catching them between the vertical rails.

At a sanctuary in Oregon where fencing is required to keep rescued horses safe, Humane Society of the United States wildlife expert Dave Pauli has created safe passageways with plastic piping for turtles, snakes, and small mammals; widened spaces atop fence sections so deer can jump over; secured lean-to posts so mountain lions and other climbers can cross; and carved out holes at midlevel that foxes can pass through.

On properties with no pets or other domestic animals to contain, hedgerows are a natural alternative to fencing, providing privacy for people and even more habitat for wild neighbors.

THE HUMANE GARDENER

Be a trash collector.

It's hard for many of us to resist the last spoonful of peanut butter, but for raccoons, skunks, and even bears, the temptation to investigate food containers can turn deadly when hands or limbs become stuck. Yogurt cups with angled rims are particularly problematic, catching the heads of skunks unable to pull them off. Dispose of these and other unwanted items—including fishing line, which jams the intestinal tracts of birds—in secured trash bins.

Time your tree trimming.

Countless squirrels, raccoons, and birds are displaced when gardeners and landscapers cut down trees during nesting season. Before pruning or removing vegetation, check for signs of habitation, or better yet, wait until after leaves have fallen and families have moved on. If you inadvertently displace a nest of squirrels or birds, put the babies in a wicker basket or similar container; hang it from a branch or attach it to the tree trunk out of direct sunlight and monitor from a distance.

A little patience will go a long way toward protecting these robins, who spend about two weeks in the nest before fledging. Check vegetation before pruning by watching for parent activity and listening for the sounds of baby animals. Careful observation can prevent displacement. Nests of lichen-covered hummingbirds blend into bark and foliage, while those of hooded orioles in the Southwest can be hidden on the underside of palm fronds.

(It's a myth that parents will reject babies who've been handled by humans.) If you see no signs of the parents' return, call a wildlife rehabilitator for further assistance.

Don't bird-nap.

Juvenile animals experience streaks of independence at an early age; birds test their wings as parents keep watch, fawns hide in vegetation while does forage, and young bobcats explore while their mother hunts for food or moves siblings one at a time to another den site. "She doesn't have a station wagon," says Linda Searles, executive director of the Southwest Wildlife Conservation Center in Scottsdale, Arizona. "She can't load up all of her kittens and drive them to wherever she wants to move to."

Yet well-intentioned citizens regularly scoop up young wildlife and bring them to already burdened rehabilitation centers. Before you create an orphan unnecessarily, consult humanesociety.org/wildneighbors or call a wildlife rehabilitator to determine whether a rescue is truly warranted.

Keep bird feeders clean.

Feeding birds helps connect people with nature, but does it help birds? Researchers' attempts to answer that question have elicited conflicting results. Some studies show that supplemental feeding increases winter survival and enhances spring breeding, while others conclude it can lower reproductive success.[2] And when examined alongside habitat elements present across multiple urban yards, feeders were found to make no difference in native species richness, whereas trees and berrying plants had a noticeable positive impact.[3]

Orphaned bobcats (top) and other species require intensive care to stay healthy without becoming too acclimated to humans. It's best to leave young animals in the wild, where parents often continue to feed them and impart crucial survival skills long after they're old enough to wander. Birds bring treats to fledglings in the trees, and does hide their fawns in thick vegetation while foraging. The presence of juvenile animals in your yard is often no cause for alarm, but a few clues—lack of feathers, closed eyes, inability to hop or move—can help you decide if they need your assistance.

If you provide seed for birds, clean feeders frequently to prevent the spread of disease.

Enclosed outdoor spaces keep cats safe and also protect wildlife.

You can't go wrong by adding native trees and shrubs, but if you want to supplement winter food supplies, be aware of the potential for disease transmission. Feeders have been implicated in the spread of salmonellosis among pine siskins in California and mycoplasmosis among house finches in the eastern United States. "They often end up being blinded by this," says Lynn Miller, who has treated infected

THE HUMANE GARDENER

finches at the HSUS's Cape Wildlife Center in Barnstable, Mass. "They'll just sit there and huddle on the ground or on a feeder."

Minimize harm by washing feeders with a 10 percent bleach solution once a week. Change water in birdbaths daily, removing debris with a scrub brush.

Herd cats.

They're often blamed for killing wildlife, but ultimately, cats are outside through no fault of their own. Life is tough for them, too, as they face traffic, toxic substances, and people with ill intentions. Welcome cats to the great indoors by creating habitat that appeals to their instincts as both a predator and prey species. Add ramps and shelving on walls to form a cat superhighway, cat trees to indulge their desire to climb, and tunnels and toys to keep them stimulated. Retrofit a deck or patio into a "catio," or push a table next to a windowsill and add a bed to create the perfect luxury box seat for bird-watching.

Making the world safer for animals isn't just the purview of wildlife rescuers; it's the responsibility of everyone with a patch of grass and a conscience. Animals continue to succumb to mowers and car wheels, but thanks to the young man who saved him and the rehabilitators who pieced him back together, City Wildlife's American toad patient recovered. With his body healed just in time for hibernation, he was expected to live a normal life on three legs after being released at his old stomping grounds—where, with any luck, he'll now be protected by people on the lookout for the safety of all the creatures quietly journeying through their backyards.

Along the shorelines of Ontario's Big Bay Point, Jennifer Howard has advocated for animals in wetlands destined to become resorts and ball fields. She's successfully lobbied for turtle crossing signs to encourage drivers to slow down. She's added ponds in her backyard to create more habitat and turned her bathtub into a way station for injured turtles in need of overnight care en route to wildlife rehabilitators.

Just as human neighbors see Howard as a go-to person for helping wildlife in distress, animals seek refuge in her garden. With the help of her camera, she tracks their journeys through her community. What she documents isn't always pretty. Sometimes it's gruesome. But her work makes people think, demonstrating not just what's being lost at human hands but what can, with a little more effort and mindfulness, be brought back from the brink.

Jennifer Howard

wildlife rescuer and activist

*A small backyard sanctuary in rapidly
developing Innisfil, Ontario*

Picked up by neighbors who assumed he was orphaned, Baby,
the cedar waxwing, eventually rejoined his kind in the wild after
Howard found a family who accepted him.

THE HUMANE GARDENER

It was Jennifer Howard's last chance to find a home for the young cedar waxwing she called Baby. Brought to her by well-meaning neighbors who thought he was orphaned, the bird had likely just been testing his wings. But after feeding him for days and searching fruitlessly for his family, Howard grew increasingly concerned. As she became attached to Baby, she feared he'd soon become bonded to her, too.

Lifting Baby's cage from her car at a local arboretum where she'd decided to release him, Howard was nervous. But she needn't have worried. Soon Baby began singing, and a family in the trees responded. The adults swooped down to check him out. "And I opened the cage and I felt like, well, once I do this, I'm not in control anymore," Howard says. "And they took him right in. He went right up into the tree with the other fledglings because they were all calling. I had tears in my eyes."

Fifteen minutes later, a fierce thunderstorm rolled through, and Howard raced back to the site, worried for Baby's safety. She called out to the fledgling. "And I heard him calling, and he came flying down, and he landed on me," she says. "And then he flew up onto the tree where the food was, had a little bit of a nibble, and then he flew off to the parents again."

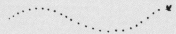

Baby's rehoming provided a moment of relief in an otherwise heart-breaking era for wildlife along the shores of Lake Simcoe, where the development of a new resort has displaced longtime forest inhabitants. "Everything's being uprooted," says Howard. "We had a moose on the front lawn."

Billed as the largest of its kind in North America, the resort is marketed to prospective buyers as a way to "escape for a little 'me' time in your own private hideaway." The extravagant human habitat has replaced thousands of trees, including the endangered butternut, in an area Howard had surveyed for a breeding bird census project in the early 2000s. As a teenager, her son Jeff found an endangered Blanding's turtle on a bike ride through the woods. "I know exactly what life was in there," Howard says. "They've destroyed wetlands. It's broken my heart. It's prompted me to make my garden even bigger and better and more natural so there's lots of food sources for everything that passes through here."

Howard has grown familiar with the needs of the region's wild species through her photography and involvement in citizen science programs. Working with conservation agencies and nonprofits, she has tracked the comings and goings of loons, woodcocks, snakes, bald eagles, redheaded woodpeckers, and many other animals in her garden and community. She has learned about the importance of native plants and the impact of invasive species through participation in a marsh biological survey. Her photos of mass die-offs of fish and birds on a local beach, along with her outreach and rescue efforts, led to "watershed hero" and education awards from the Lake Simcoe Region Conservation Authority and Ontario Nature.

Howard's meticulous documentation of at-risk species, combined with her ability to build relationships with everyone from town road crews to provincial conservation organizations, was the driving force behind municipal approval of turtle crossing signs in more than a

A year after Howard
worked with the Toronto
Wildlife Centre to
treat three fox kits with
mange, one showed
up again at the old den
site by the lakefront,
napping and playing
while Howard watched
from a distance.

half dozen sites. A quiet determination underlies her approach to her photography and gardening as well. Whether she's watching a Canada darner dragonfly laying eggs in one of her three backyard ponds or a mother mink teaching her young how to eat crayfish at the nearby lake, she maintains a respectful distance. Rather than engaging in the baiting and harassing she's seen other photographers employ to get their best shot, she simply waits. "It's sheer patience," she says. "It's taken me years to get some of the photographs I've gotten—twenty years for some of them."

The animals in Howard's backyard are happy to oblige. Warblers land right in front of her to wash up and take a sip from a low cement birdbath. Chipmunks pop their heads out of the soil in winter, and great crested flycatchers nest in the screech owl box, which visiting screech owls seem to ignore. In the three brush piles Howard constructed, Carolina wrens go to sleep. Dead trees are left standing to provide food and refuge for brown creepers and woodpeckers, who also feast on the grubs in a decades-old stump where a wood frog hangs out. Bright orange jewelweed flowers nourish hummingbirds, and volunteer sumacs, coral honeysuckles, and dogwoods beckon berry eaters. Elderberries planted recently by Howard draw flocks of cedar waxwings to her yard, and skunks, toads, a great horned owl, and a fox family have come to visit.

One year raccoon babies frolicked atop the arbor above the ponds, yawning and stretching and passing out. "And Mama would be there," says Howard. "They'd start gnawing at her ear, pulling on her tail— I mean, the abuse you take!" Howard reveled in their nightly antics,

A black squirrel prepares a mushroom feast in Howard's garden. In addition to planting acorns, squirrels also contribute to forest regeneration by dispersing spores of fungi that trees depend on for nutrient and water transfer.

Chipmunks find warmth underground in Howard's winter garden, where they have access to a pond as well as a large cement birdbath placed low "so the chippies and everybody else can get a drink of fresh water."

Orphaned at a vulnerable age, these raccoons learned to survive with the help of Howard and the natural habitat she has created.

Northern flickers and other cavity nesters raise their young in large trees and snags. Old tree stumps and logs in the garden shelter wood frogs and other amphibians.

THE HUMANE GARDENER

A wild turkey struts his stuff for some nearby females on the front lawn. Squirrels and birds dine on crabapples, elderberries, and other fruiting shrubs and trees in Howard's yard.

until one day the babies appeared by themselves. Old enough to eat but too young to survive on their own, they adopted Howard as a surrogate when she learned the wildlife rehabilitation facility was too full. She carefully helped them make their way around the ponds and taught them how to be raccoons until they were old enough to leave and find their own dens for the winter.

With the help of wildlife rehabilitators, she has also saved foxes, owls, and a goose with fishing line wrapped around one leg. "They just seem to come to me," she says. "They need your help sometimes. They need your compassion. It's not their fault they're here in the first place, and it's not their fault they don't have a home. There's more and more habitat disappearing every day, and that's our habitat, too."

CHAPTER 5

A Harvest for All: Share the Bounty Through Peaceful Coexistence

---

*Animals aren't out to get us, but the "pest"-control industry
would have us believe otherwise.*

My childhood nature collection was an odd reflection of my won-
derment at worlds both natural and artificial: fish teeth from a
North Carolina beach, fluorescent-dyed corals from a Maryland gift
shop, and—the pièce de résistance—a postcard from Shenandoah
National Park depicting an animal who'd attained mythical status
for me.

The caption told the tale of a triumphant comeback: "By the early
nineteen-thirties, the Virginia Deer had been eliminated from the
northern Blue Ridge Mountains. Under Park Service protection since
1935 it has returned in great numbers to this area that is so well suited
to its needs."

Back then I would have been thrilled by just one sighting. Today
the yellowing souvenir has a different meaning, epitomizing our
constantly changing attitude toward other species. It would be
hard to find such unqualified celebrations of white-tailed deer now,
nearly four decades after I stored my ten-cent treasure in that over-
stuffed shoe box.

Victims of centuries of misunderstanding, deer have undergone dramatic population swings in my own state since as early as 1729; that year, their numbers were so low that Maryland colonial authorities banned winter hunting from January through July. Since then, in many states across the country, they've been nearly shot out of existence again and again, only to be transported across regions and "restocked" repeatedly to let the cycle begin anew.[1]

Pick any number of wild species—wolves, prairie dogs, Canada geese, turkeys, mountain lions, even eastern gray squirrels—and the narrative is wearyingly the same. In the mid-1700s, bounties were placed on squirrel heads for the offense of eating corn; so many Pennsylvania hunters collected on an offer of three pence per scalp that the colony's treasury was depleted. Scarcely a century later, the rodents went from being reviled to revered, and squirrels were imported into urban centers up and down the East Coast for the amusement of citizens who fed them by hand and put up nest boxes for their young. Transported farther afield to Seattle and London, they're now blamed for marginalizing native squirrel species.[2]

The current objects of our collective disdain, white-tailed deer, are also accused of causing a host of ills, from Lyme disease to garden demolition to loss of forest undergrowth. But as is often the case, the story is much more complex.

The black-legged tick, which spreads the Lyme-causing bacterium, makes itself at home on the bodies of more than sixty species of mammals and birds, not just deer.[3] And while deer eat their fair share of vegetation in gardens and natural environments, they are one of countless influential organisms in a vast and largely unknown network. Even the voracious appetite of the tiny earthworm, long revered

Encapsulating our contradictory relationship with animals, this postcard from my childhood celebrated the comeback of a species nearly shot out of existence.

Canada geese are one of many species subjected to large population swings at the hands of humans. After being hunted to near-extinction, they were transported in the mid-twentieth century beyond their historic range in an attempt to "restock" them for hunters. In the decades since, they've thrived in mowed landscapes that provide easy escape routes to ponds and lakes for nesting parents. Planting more natural vegetation is a proven solution to human-goose conflict, but some communities still call in the big guns, resulting in government-sponsored mass gassing in improvised euthanasia chambers.

by gardeners, may be dramatically altering life in and above the soil; in northern forests where the last glacial ice sheet extended, no earthworms existed until they were introduced from Europe and Asia. Very efficient at what they do, these leaf-chomping recyclers process the spongy duff layer too quickly for plants accustomed to living among slowly decomposing leaves. The loss of this rich organic material also affects animals like ovenbirds, forest inhabitants who build nests in fallen leaves and have lower breeding rates in areas with high concentrations of earthworms.[4]

The cascade effects of so many creatures—some native, others not, some known, others not yet discovered—make our tendency to zero in on a single species shortsighted at best, especially when the effectiveness of existing deer management programs is so understudied, notes wildlife biologist John Hadidian, author of *Wild Neighbors: The Humane Approach to Living with Wildlife.* "Why are we scapegoating deer when we have billions—literally billions—of worms working to change that forest ecology?" he asks. "You've got to look at an entire system and see what's going on above and below ground before you begin to make judgments about what needs to happen."

While the prevalence of deer may seem novel, our view is distorted by the "abnormally unbrowsed forest" conditions that set the stage for much of the research on eastern forest ecology in the twentieth century, writes biologist David George Haskell. "Historical and archaeological information…all points to the same conclusion: deer were plentiful inhabitants of our forests before guns removed them in the 1800s," he concludes in his book *The Forest Unseen: A Year's Watch in Nature.* "The deerless forests of the early and middle 1900s were aberrations."

Regardless of the science behind deer management programs, targeting these animals is big business. The number one source of revenue for state wildlife agencies, deer are also a boon to local communities that profit from tourism dollars during hunting season. That money trail may explain why, paradoxically, those who advocated twenty years ago for expanded deer hunts based on lack of natural controls have changed their tune: now that coyotes and mountain lions are ready and willing to take on the job of apex predators, some hunters and government officials have argued they won't leave enough deer for humans to kill. In the eyes of our shortsighted species, it seems that carnivores, too, must meet their demise for just doing what comes naturally to them—and the blame casting starts again.

Cultural biases fueling these broad-scale responses to the presence of wildlife too often influence the decisions we make in our own homes and gardens. A widespread disconnection from the natural world, fueled by fearmongering by the "pest"-control industry, obscures the many effective ways of coexisting with the creatures in our midst. The results can be tragic for animals simply trying to survive: people still shoot opossums because they don't like their appearance. They pour gasoline down mole holes, set body-gripping traps for groundhogs, and trap and relocate animals in unfamiliar territories, often to their inevitable doom. They call in "nuisance" wildlife control operators who have been known to do all these things and worse.

John Griffin, director of urban wildlife solutions for the Humane Society of the United States, came upon one such devastating scene while responding to a call about raccoons living in the chimney of a

Revered by Native Americans but then persecuted for centuries on the western range, coyotes are filling an ecological niche vacated after wolf populations were decimated. We could learn from their ability to coexist among us.

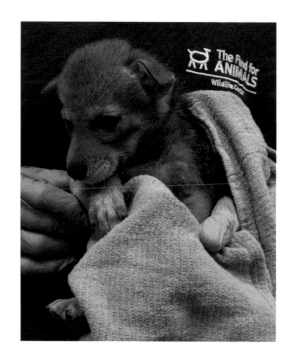

A wildlife rehabilitation center cared for this coyote pup and five siblings whose parents were shot on a private property in California.

suburban home. Griffin and his colleague had planned to use humane eviction methods to help the mother move her family along peacefully to another den site. But just before they arrived, the homeowners decided they didn't want to pay for the service and took matters into their own hands by setting a fire in the fireplace below. Intending to chase out their unwanted guests, they didn't realize the kits, only four to six weeks old, were still too young to climb.

"They essentially cooked on the smoke shelf," says Griffin. By the time he arrived, the mom was lying at the top of the chimney, holding in her mouth the one baby she'd managed to carry out. "She was really impacted. I'm not just being anthropomorphic. It was really signs of mourning to me. I've seen it," says Griffin, who used to work at a primate facility. "I remember seeing rhesus macaques mourning babies, carrying dead babies around for weeks—moms who had a miscarriage or something that happened to their baby when they were born. The mom raccoon was out during the day, just dragging this baby around, uncertain about what to do."

Her painful fate could have been easily avoided. With the chimney flue already closed, the house was never even accessible to the raccoons. "People do terrible things out there—they've got a problem, and they take it personally," Griffin says. "It's typically framed as: 'This is a nuisance. This animal is targeting me in some way; it's after me. I've got to solve it, and I've got to solve it on an emergency basis'—without really thinking about what's going on."

In his work to help communities humanely address wildlife conflicts, Griffin often encounters the grisly aftermath of other rash human behaviors: a colony of bats poisoned by a mixture of fumigation foggers and other pesticides, a squirrel left to die of stress and starvation in a live trap forgotten in an attic, another squirrel lying squashed in a body-crushing device on a roof. Sometimes the perpetrators are homeowners themselves; other times they are hired operators who've left a trail of destruction in their wake.

Though typically marketed as "humane," traditional services either trap and kill—often by suffocation, drowning, or poisons—or relocate wildlife. While the latter method sounds preferable, animals who survive the stress of transport will likely face a different kind of death sentence, competing for resources and struggling to avoid predation in unfamiliar territories. And any dependent young back in their home range will wait helplessly for a mother who never returns.

Part of a multibillion-dollar industry that prioritizes profit over animal welfare, these companies promote misunderstandings of natural behavior and have little incentive to address the real sources of conflict. Usually commanding a fee for each animal trapped, they catch as many as they can, without regard for whether they've captured the animal in question or what made the situation so attractive to wildlife in the first place. Preying on a lack of customer knowledge about urban ecology, many pest-control services leave the real issue—a hole in a roof, an accessible shed, an open vent—unaddressed and destined to invite more trouble. Even worse, they seal up entry points while mothers are out foraging, a cruel fate for the family and one that can lead desperate moms to shred whatever repairs have been made.

Because they profit off homeowner anxieties, it's in their financial interest to exacerbate unfounded fears. On a typical website, a photo of an obviously frightened opossum baring her teeth serves as a scare tactic, even though the species is among the most gentle and beneficial in the garden. "Possums are pests," reads the accompanying text. "They eat your pet's food, they crawl into your shed or under your deck or in your attic, and they live there and poop there and make a stink there. They scavange [sic] your garbage, and they are common city animals. Heck, lots of people just don't like the way they look."[5]

Media contribute to a dominant cultural narrative that reads like a wartime propaganda playbook: "Aggressive coyotes terrorize northeast side neighborhood," warns one Tucson news outlet. "Geese be gone: Plan calls for dogs to rid Mall of fowl that befoul," reads a flippant headline in Washington, DC. In one particularly bizarre "investigative" report, Pittsburgh newscasters chastise an animal control agency that has finally stopped indiscriminately trapping and killing up to

1,500 raccoons a year—not to mention groundhogs and opossums—from the yards of anyone requesting the service.[6]

Manufacturers of all manner of weaponry stand ready to capitalize on popular stereotypes, encouraging homeowners to spear moles with harpoon traps for eating grubs in the lawn or to gas ground squirrels for digging burrows. Like the shoddy work of many commercial providers, do-it-yourself battles can have unintended consequences for a range of species. Pets are collateral damage of rodenticides meant for voles and traps intended for coyotes. Birds and squirrels get stuck in glue traps set outside to catch mice; at City Wildlife, staff have cared for a variety of glue-trap victims: opossums, robins, snakes, brown creepers, and a cardinal who lost his crest and flight feathers trying to break free from one. "It's heartbreaking when we've got an animal brought in on a glue trap," says Paula Goldberg. "They'll get so stressed and they'll struggle so hard that they end up not only pulling off fur or feathers, but in their panic, they break their bones."

Evolution toward a more humane ethic is not just a moral imperative but also the only practical solution in an increasingly crowded world. Wherever we live, other species were there first, in spite of misinformed articles like a recent *New York Times* piece titled "Raccoons Invade Brooklyn" that implies otherwise.[7] As Hadidian points out, raccoons were already on the planet in almost modern form a million years ago. By contrast, we didn't come along as a species until eight hundred thousand years later. But we've more than compensated for our evolutionary delays. Over half the human population worldwide now lives in urban areas, and the US population is expected to increase from 314 to 400 million over the next thirty-five years. So the question must be asked: Who really invaded Brooklyn?

Javelinas, common animals in the Southwest, live in large groups to help protect their homes. Like all animals, they deserve a safe space to raise their families.

"We moved into their backyard—they didn't move into our backyard," says Linda Searles of the bobcats, coyotes, and other misunderstood animals cared for at the Southwest Wildlife Conservation Center, her Scottsdale facility. "They're really just seeking the same things that we are seeking, and that is a place to raise our family, food to eat, and companionship of our own kind."

To think differently about perceived conflict with wildlife in your domain, consider the following questions.

Is your home where their hearth is?

Raccoons and squirrels can traverse many city blocks without ever touching ground, making themselves at home in uncapped chimneys, attics, tree holes, and other cozy spots throughout urban territories. "And they certainly know these areas very well, and they've mapped them out in their heads to know where good den sites are, where good loafing spots are, where good food sites are," says Griffin. Whether those sites are man-made or natural makes little difference: "If it can support them, if it has food, if it has shelter, it doesn't matter if a human built it."

Rescind open invitations to your home by adding hardware cloth or commercial covers to vents, wire caps to chimneys, and wire mesh around spaces under decks or sheds. Seal holes in foundations and at roofline intersections, but be sure animals are out first, both for their sake and yours; mothers will stop at little to retrieve babies trapped inside. When their maternal instincts kick in, squirrels have even been known to fight off dogs and chew through metal.

Humane eviction methods ensure all babies are removed first so they can be reunited with their mothers.

A raccoon baby waits in a "reunion box" placed outside her birthplace in an attic. Wild mammals keep multiple den sites in reserve; once their young are removed, mothers can relocate them.

To ensure a humane and effective outcome for both human and wild families, Griffin has adopted the only proven model, one that he helped pioneer in the United States following training sessions with AAA Gates' Wildlife Control in Canada: after removing babies and placing them in a box near the animals' entryway, he installs a one-way door and waits for the mother to exit so she can move her young to an alternate den site. Only then is the structure secured to prevent recurrence.

Have you lost perspective—or failed to see theirs?

In a phenomenon known to psychologists as the availability cascade, we are more likely to create mountains of paranoia out of literal mole-hills, not to mention rabbit nests and goose poop, when exposed to

THE HUMANE GARDENER

media hype. The presence of one raccoon near a patio conjures an image of a "cavalcade of hungry raccoons knocking down your door," says Griffin. A coyote appearing on a sidewalk morphs into a predator on the hunt for humans and their pets.

Ignoring the reality that rabies transmission and animal attacks are extraordinarily rare—more people are killed by errant golf balls and pet dogs than by coyotes—we have an unfortunate tendency to overestimate the significance of even small-risk events. But behind every reductive tale of an animal caught in the wrong place at the wrong time are other considerations that get lost when we become trapped in our own humancentric narrative: That raccoon may be close to your home because he's enjoying a snack from your freshly filled bird feeder. The coyote may have made herself known to alert dog walkers to the presence of babies nearby.

This raccoon doesn't know the bird feeder isn't meant for him. When we see the world from the perspective of wildlife, we can resolve conflicts more humanely— in this case simply by taking the feeder in at night or permanently closing the restaurant.

"We tell people to just avoid that area for a while, let them raise their pups and move off, and then the problem will go away," says Searles. "The only time we ever have bite incidents with coyotes is typically when somebody's been feeding them. That's true for all wildlife like bears and lions and even prey species—when you feed them, they can get dependent on that, and then they'll lose their fear of people, and that's when people can get hurt, and the animal always suffers the ultimate consequences. They lose their life. So we have a saying: a fed bear is a dead bear."

Have you opened an all-you-can-eat restaurant?

Mountain lions paid the price when a Tucson-area community provided treats for deer and javelinas; the big cats inevitably gravitated to them as easy prey, scared human residents, and ended up dead at the hands of game officials, says Searles, whose facility rescued one. In the Scottsdale area, baby coyotes who had been repeatedly offered treats from golf carts and the snack bar became so accustomed to humans that one nipped at a woman's ankle, and the whole family was destroyed. "That did not have to happen," says Searles. "Coyotes are really good for golf courses because they keep the rodents in control; they keep the balance."

Bird feeders can attract mammals who don't know they're unwelcome at the table, with dire outcomes if they enter the yard of someone who'd rather shoot or trap squirrels and raccoons than change their own behavior. Simple and much more effective measures—including adjusting feeding times, offering smaller quantities of birdseed, and even shutting down the buffet—can keep mammals from becoming habituated.

Pet food also baits a range of species, including bobcats and coyotes. To protect both pets and wildlife, feed cats and dogs indoors and keep them on short leashes when you venture out. Be mindful of your own leftover food and garbage; bungee cords and animal-resistant trash cans help prevent spontaneous dinner parties.

Do you understand their social cues?

It doesn't take a biologist to see past the cynical exaggerations of animals as "aggressive" and "ferocious" when cornered or defending their young. Who among us isn't defensive when our lives are in danger or our family is threatened? Protective instincts are critical to the survival of all species, but that doesn't mean animals have it in for us. Because we've been so primed to believe otherwise, though, it's easy to misread their cues.

Poor eyesight can make javelinas appear to be charging at people, when in fact this shy desert species resembling a wild boar is more likely looking for an escape. Nearsightedness also plagues docile skunks, perpetuating the myth that they're walking time bombs. "A skunk might be waddling right to someone," says Griffin, "and they think, 'The skunk's coming after me.' But a skunk just sees a blurry object; it doesn't know what's going on." In fact, their first instinct is to run when frightened; if there's no escape route, they stamp their feet, raise their tails, and assess the threat—a mental calculation skunk expert Jerry Dragoo has seen them make before standing down. "If they don't fear for their life," says Dragoo, "they're not going to spray."

Contrary to popular belief, opossums have no way to fight back when challenged. All they can do is drool, hiss, and sway before playing dead. "That's their only defense," says Griffin. "They have fifty

Perhaps because of their poor eyesight, javelinas can be shy and easily frightened, but people often misinterpret their behavior.

An orphaned opossum learns survival skills at AWARE wildlife rehabilitation center in Atlanta. Frequent victims of abuse, North America's only marsupials could hardly be more beneficial to gardeners, eating carrion, insects, snails, slugs, and sometimes small rodents.

teeth, but they don't know how to use them in an aggressive way." Yet they are among the most abused mammals, intentionally run over, set on fire, and doused in insecticides—unfathomably cruel behaviors that pain wildlife rehabilitators like Melanie Furr, who has raised their orphans at AWARE in Atlanta: "There's nothing not to like about possums. They are so subdued, so nonaggressive. You have to really provoke an opossum to get bitten."

Opposums, skunks, and many other misunderstood animals can be surprisingly beneficial in the garden—another reason to learn to coexist with these unassuming creatures.

Keeping the peace—and your peas—in the garden

In spite of the free help wild animals provide, gardeners still go to great lengths to chase them away. Whether it's deer-resistant perennials, squirrel-proof bulb cages, or groundhog-repelling hot pepper spray, we've seen them all—and have debated endlessly over the effectiveness of products and solutions purported to create impenetrable borders around tasty flowers and vegetables.

While there's nothing inherently wrong with trying these more humane deterrents, they're often implemented in a vacuum, without accounting for the barren spaces that exist just outside the typical vegetable or flower patch in American suburbia. A winterberry holly in a garden near a natural woodlot may go untouched, while one in a new development with scarce habitat may be eaten to the ground. And just because an animal nibbles on one kind of plant doesn't mean she'll mow down the rest. "Every situation is unique, not to mention every animal is an individual. They all have their particular quirks and personalities," says Hadidian. "Your yard is part of a larger environment. And it's not like deer are coming into your living room and eating your couch. They're just trying to make a living."

As animals adapt to our growing presence, we can learn to better adapt to theirs. Instead of jumping to conclusions and relying on cookie-cutter solutions, use these principles to tailor your approach.

Put it in context.

When we've initiated a blame game against various species for stealing the fruits of our labor, it can be humbling to learn how wrong we may have been. The half-eaten tomato in the vegetable garden that started a war on groundhogs could have been the handiwork of a box turtle just passing through. The toppled rosebush that launched a search for an imaginary beaver was likely the fault of the gardener who added too much mulch and created a perfect habitat for voles.

What gardeners may see as arbitrary destruction is often part of a larger plan. Tree squirrels are frequent diggers in part because they must constantly regulate stowed food supplies. "One of the big misconceptions is that their behavior just seems so random, that they're just out there popping around," says Wilkes University professor Michael Steele, author of *North American Tree Squirrels*. "And the thing [people] have to realize is that just about every minute of every day is a careful behavioral decision that they're making in order to survive." Squirrels evaluate seeds to learn which are better eaten immediately and which can be stored underground. They excise embryos of fast-germinating white oak acorns to keep buried seeds from sprouting. They remember cache sites, monitoring and relocating food throughout the season. And in case any potential seed robbers are watching, eastern gray squirrels even engage in "deceptive caching," says

Steele, digging a hole and pretending to bury a seed they keep in their mouths—a type of maneuver previously thought to occur only in primates.

Make animals your allies.

The hidden talents of these animals are best-kept secrets the pest-control and conventional landscaping companies don't want you to know about—for good reason. From foxes and hawks who keep rodents in check to blue jays and squirrels who plant trees that nourish and shelter hundreds of species, our hardworking wild neighbors could put these industries out of business if only we let them.

Part of nature's cleanup crew, opossums eat carrion, rotting fruit, and also many insects, including Lyme-carrying ticks. Skunks feast on grubs in the ground and insects that congregate on garden plants. "If you've got a tomato worm on your tomato plants, that will probably do more damage to your crops than a skunk would," says Dragoo. "If a skunk has a choice between a tomato and a tomato worm, it'll go after the tomato worm."

Skunks were once so helpful to farmers, in fact, that New York hop growers were the driving force behind state legislation to protect them. But that was before the chemical age obscured animals' important role as farm and garden helpers. To nurture these wild partners, we need to protect the food supply in the soil, where many insects begin their lives as tasty larvae. "The birds and the mammals, they're dependent on these creatures," says *Life in the Soil* author Jim Nardi. "I have a lot of shrews in my backyard—they're wonderful little guys, and they feed on these insects in the soil. And if the soil's poisoned, there's nothing for them to feed upon."

Because of their voracious appetite for grubs, skunks are so helpful in the garden that farmers once sought legal protections for them.

Considered "ecosystem engineers," burrowing animals provide excellent tilling services. Research has shown that grasslands with resident prairie dogs support a greater diversity of plant and animal life.

Burrowing animals like prairie dogs return buried nutrients to the surface where plant roots are located, giving them a dose of natural fertilizer. Moles eat more than half their body weight each day, aerating the soil while dining on earthworms and other invertebrates—a workload that's been likened to a man pushing an elephant out of a tunnel with one hand in twenty minutes. In the United Kingdom, their industrious habits have also been shown to create fertile ground for host plants that support rare butterfly larvae, while in my own yard each morning, molehills draw curious birds who inspect them for turned-up treats.

Let them eat plants.

It may sound counterintuitive, but the more vegetation you share, the more productive and conflict-free your garden will be. Resistance to wild visitors is often futile anyway, as many diversify their menus based on availability. It's more rewarding and effective to grow a little extra for sharing than to waste time trying to subvert hungry creatures.

On my property, rabbits keep dandelions in check, even chowing down on the seeds, and deer and groundhogs provide pruning assistance in the crowded sassafras and staghorn sumac groves we let root into the turfgrass. When planted near vegetable gardens, hedgerows of native shrubs and wildflowers provide gathering places for nesting birds and other wild garden helpers, including pollinators who also prey on aphids and other crop-nibbling insects.

When animals inevitably snack on things not intended for them, observant gardeners adjust the menu. Squirrels won't leave any corn for Nardi to harvest, so he grows a bounty of dozens of other crops

Who needs herbicides when we have rabbits? Dandelions and other lawn weeds are their favorite delicacies.

It's their world, too: share the bounty by planting a little extra for wild friends.

Seeded and later eaten by birds, common evening primrose deters Japanese beetles (left) from feeding on nearby vegetation. While a bumblebee extracts nectar and spreads pollen in the process, a carpenter bee engages in "nectar robbery" (above left), drilling a hole in the flower's base for easier access.

instead. Some gardeners employ strategic planting and harvesting methods to ensure there's enough to go around: Leave fruit at the tops of trees for birds, and they'll also dine on insects eating your crops. Plant radishes for flea beetles, and they'll likely abandon their potato and eggplant snack for their favorite meal. In my garden, Japanese beetles congregate on the common evening primrose, content to leave everything else alone as long as I cultivate this preferred delicacy.

Redirect their attention.

Plants can also serve as repellents: Lavender keeps deer from devouring carrots and beets, and anise hyssop can protect tomatoes from grazing mammals. While some gardeners sprinkle hot pepper around their plants, I grow cayenne peppers on the borders of my vegetable gardens. Not surprisingly, no one but me seems to want to touch them.

When shopping for commercial repellents, exercise caution; some marketed as humane are anything but. Predator urine, sold as a natural way to scare off wild visitors, is collected from coyotes, foxes, and other animals raised in wire cages on fur farms.[8] Adopt a dog and enlist her help in marking your territory instead, or make your project even more DIY: Every couple of weeks in the summer, I ask my husband to go on pee patrol—an effective, free-range, and locally sourced way to protect joe-pye weed and other plants from being nibbled on so they can grow tall enough for the butterflies to enjoy.

Other temporary deterrents include reflective flash tape and motion-detection sprinklers, which gently startle animals enough to encourage them to move along. Fencing made of stakes and welded wire is a more foolproof way to protect new gardens and young trees until they are tall enough to withstand mammalian snacking.

Bars of smelly soap in old, cut-up laundry bags effectively deterred deer from nibbling our meadow garden so there would still be enough blooms for the butterflies. A fritillary enjoyed sipping from the mesh after a rain.

In permanently fenced areas, L-shaped footers—wire mesh buried a foot deep and extending out horizontally by another foot—can keep groundhogs and other tunneling animals from crawling underneath.[9] Use these options sparingly, and be sure your choice of fencing material won't ensnare animals.

By employing a combination of methods unique to your site and the animals who visit, you can learn to coexist with wildlife and even enjoy the magic they bring. "A lot of people say, 'I've got a skunk in my backyard; what do I do?" says Dragoo. "And my advice is to get a lawn chair, pour a beer, put your feet up, and watch it because it's very entertaining. If it's not causing a problem, then why do you want to remove it?"

More often than not, coexistence requires only a simple attitude adjustment about what constitutes a problem in the first place. Reactions to animals can be so reflexively negative that even squirrels and blue jays visiting bird feeders during times of late-winter scarcity are chased away—not a fine how-do-you-do for little creatures who provide more sustenance to birds than any feeder ever could. By planting acorns and other nuts, these forest regenerators ensure a steady food supply for many of their wild brethren; oaks alone feed more caterpillars, the mainstay of baby bird food, than anything else in the garden.

In the end, all of our backyard visitors bring many more gifts than they take away. If we're patient enough to observe them and flexible enough to accept them, they may eventually grow enough seeds, berries, and nuts to feed us all.

As ecologists work to reverse man-made damage to natural areas, we gardeners have an opportunity to bring back habitat in places where those natural areas are already long gone. The age of turfgrass lined by thin woods may have created a welcome mat for deer and other species, but that doesn't mean they'll find enough to eat upon arrival. Instead of becoming angry with them for trying to eke out a meal or two, gardeners and farmers like Tammi Hartung take a more compassionate approach, adding plants especially for animals and gently steering them away from crops not featured on the menu. The rock squirrels sometimes eat her birdseed, and the dozens of resident deer occasionally nibble her berry bushes, but Hartung still manages to raise hundreds of crops for herself and her business. Providing their own weeding and insect control services, the animals bring natural balance and unexpected joy. They are not intruders but partners, she says, inextricable from the landscape: "They've just become a part of it all."

**THE HUMANE
GARDENER**

Tammi Hartung

herbalist; flower and vegetable farmer

THE HOME

Desert Canyon Farm, Cañon City, Colorado

A herd of about thirty deer inhabit Desert Canyon Farm, which benefits from the animals' preference for invasive bindweed. The deer also nibble in the hedgerows and on garden scraps under the "giveaway tree" in the back of the property.

THE HUMANE GARDENER

When Tammi Hartung picks the last tomatoes of the season, warblers keep her company, snacking on aphids covering the waning plants nearby. As she harvests her coveted raspberries, curve-billed thrashers come even closer, perching on the fence to politely request their share. "They don't really bother those fruits normally on their own," says Hartung, "but they sit there waiting for me to toss one, and they catch it, and off they go."

Eventually the thrashers will return the favor, hopping alongside Hartung's husband to provide free garden help. "They know that wherever Chris goes, there's likely going to be some soil disturbed or something happening that will produce an insect," says Hartung, "so they follow him around."

The birds are among many willing assistants on Desert Canyon Farm, where the Hartungs grow food and herbs for themselves, potted plants for sale, and crops for a flower seed company. Toads and frogs snack on slugs and pill bugs, while red-winged blackbirds eat squash bugs, beetles, and grasshoppers. Gambel's quail wander from their home base under a cholla cactus to nibble on ants and gnats in the greenhouse or peck at crickets and earwigs among the lettuce and spinach. Foxes roam throughout the five-acre property to provide free rodent control.

Animals are so welcome here that Hartung adds fencing not to protect her plants but to ensure the safety of her wild friends. "Years ago I made raised beds out of cinder block, and we had them for years, and the deer never had trouble," she says. "But there was a doe a buck was pursuing, and she ran through them and broke her hind leg in one of those cinder blocks."

Nursing two fawns at the time, the doe eventually recovered with the help of state wildlife agents, who put a radio collar on her to track her progress. Now about twelve years old and walking with a permanent limp, the deer, dubbed Radio Collar Mom, is "the matriarch of our herd," Hartung says. "And she's old, but she's totally in charge—of everything and everyone. We've watched her chase big dogs—down the middle of our road for blocks—that were bothering the deer."

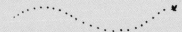

The Hartungs still prefer to have as few walls between themselves and nature as possible. Aside from the fence added to protect deer from further injury in the cinder-block garden, an electric fence keeps bears from raiding the beehive, and an enclosure around the bird garden safeguards feeders. The farm is otherwise open to all who want to pass through, including foxes, skunks, and a mountain lion caught

Walking around the farm one day, Tammi Hartung caught sight of a buck nibbling on sunflower seed heads before casually making his way through the greenhouse (left). Security cameras have revealed a fox (above) and a mountain lion providing rodent control services and, in this case, napping.

THE HUMANE GARDENER

The Hartungs' vegetable garden is one of the few spots where a barrier
has been erected between plants and animals—but only to help
keep the animals safe after a deer injured her leg in the cinder blocks.
She has recovered and is now the matriarch of the herd.

Curve-billed thrashers nest in cholla cactus (left). Hartung's desert garden of native southwestern plants (below) is also home to Gambel's quail, sharp-shinned hawks, gray-crowned rosy finches, rabbits, and a fox.

by a wildlife camera moving through the greenhouses. "We've made our farm a nature preserve and a wildlife habitat," says Hartung. "So we've intentionally welcomed them in, which means then I have to find a way to protect things they are going to forage on or destroy in some fashion, without putting up barriers if I can help it."

Hartung had plenty of practice for life in the cultivated wilds of Cañon City, located minutes away from federal lands where a range of large species roam. After marrying Chris Hartung in 1994, she moved to the seven-hundred-acre historic farmstead he managed for the Denver Botanic Gardens, where frequent public traffic made fencing inappropriate, even when a much hungrier array of guests, from coyotes to deer to cottontails, came calling. "And I just planted my garden in this naive way, thinking that nothing was going to bother it," says Hartung. "So then it was a matter of trying to figure out ways to have the wildlife around because we really enjoyed that. At the same time I wanted to have my vegetables and my herbs."

Three decades later, wild animals are so critical to the success of Desert Canyon that their role in pollination and natural insect control is codified in the farm's organic certification by the US Department of Agriculture. Buffer zones of vegetation protect the edge of the property from external pesticides and are formally recognized as wildlife habitat—official validation that buoys the Hartungs' request that county crews leave dead trees standing for downy woodpeckers, flickers, and cavity-nesting bees.

With so many hungry diners in their midst, it seems there wouldn't be enough food left for the Hartungs and their customers. But patient observation of animal behavior has helped Hartung provide enough habitat for all the species on-site, including her own. When squirrels chewed through the emitters of Hartung's irrigation lines, she realized they were thirsty and put out plates of water for them. "So often what I've learned is that we jump to these conclusions about what's happening, and that's not what's really going on at all," she says. "We thought for years that deer were eating crops, and we were doing our defensive moves on individual crops. And then we started paying more attention, and we noticed that they weren't eating those at all." The plant of choice was invasive bindweed—"our biggest problem here" in the pathways along the one-hundred-foot beds. Because of the deer herd's help in controlling the unwanted plant, Chris now

THE HUMANE GARDENER

rototills only once or twice a year, says Hartung, "and the rest of the time the deer move through the field, and that's what they eat."

Trained as an herbalist and propagator, Hartung makes extensive use of plants to both welcome and deter wildlife. When birds started feasting on raspberries—Hartung's favorite fruit—she added a row of sunflowers next to the bushes as an alternative for them. She intersperses peppermint plants among squash to repel snacking rodents, chives among strawberries to deter deer, and extra rows of parsley so deer and rabbits avoid her salad greens in favor of the tastier herb.

A "giveaway tree" in the back of the farm, where Hartung puts vegetable scraps, fallen fruit, and other discards from the garden, provides a routine dining spot for deer, skunks, and raccoons. "Most

Chocolate flower (right) and Bush's coneflower (left) are among the dozens of crops grown each year for a seed company, bringing a diversity of pollinators to the farm. The Hartungs also grow hundreds of other species in their fields, gardens, orchards, pollinator hedgerows, and greenhouses.

wildlife are creatures of habit," she says. "They go where they went the day before, and they keep going back as long as it's advantageous for them to do that, and if you can just figure out a way to break the cycle, then they tend to find another route."

Caution tape has helped guard potted strawberries and penstemons, and a Scaredy Cat motion sprinkler temporarily protects pumpkins, corn, and bird feeders from raccoon nibblers. "I don't leave those kinds of things up," says Hartung. "[Animals] get used to it, and it's not effective anymore."

. · · . · · · · · · · · · · · · · ·. ➤

Friendliness to wild inhabitants was a trait not initially shared by their human neighbors, but the Hartungs' kind example seems to be catching on. Most neighbors have stopped spraying their lawns with chemicals. They're more tolerant of deer, adding fencing around their vegetable gardens. And one longtime cattle rancher recently asked Hartung what she does about cottontails and jackrabbits, citing his wife's annoyance at their burgeoning populations. When she suggested he let the foxes, coyotes, and bobcats take care of them, he said, "I've been telling the guys at the ranch to shoot any of those things they see. Maybe I should rethink that."

Desert Canyon Farm was a wounded landscape mostly devoid of plant life when the Hartungs moved there in 1996, but it's now filled with plants that provide food and shelter for wildlife, including hawthorns, honey locusts, sycamores, cottonwoods, roses, currants, chokeberries, wild plums, mahonia, lilacs, and New Mexico privet. Borders and rows overflowing with herbs and perennials—lavender, penstemons, chocolate flowers, fennel, curry plant, coneflowers,

Though initially concerned about sharp-shinned hawks' propensity to eat small birds, Hartung quickly came to her senses, she says, recognizing their important role in managing populations of mice, rabbits, and squirrels. "He only eats what he needs," she noted on her blog of one frequent hawk visitor, "unlike many of us humans."

TAMMI HARTUNG

milkweeds, hollyhocks, rue, savory, skullcaps, and many other of the fifty to sixty perennial crops grown each year for a German seed company—bring an abundance of pollinators.

Ponds originally added for irrigation have also become oases for fish, red-eared slider turtles, frogs, salamanders, a grey heron, and a white-faced ibis. Even the bird feeders have added unexpected food sources. When an adult pair of foxes began stopping beneath the Hartungs' bird feeders with their kits, night cameras revealed they were eating mice drawn to the seed. Much to Tammi's delight, they were also moving through the greenhouse, sleeping under the benches, and playing tag over her daughter's car.

During a playful showdown when Hartung tried to scare a raccoon away from a bird feeder, he just looked at her and kept eating. That night Hartung installed a motion-detecting sprinkler, one of her favorite humane deterrents. "That took care of it," she says, laughing at the memory. "He's a character."

CHAPTER 6

The Gift that Keeps On Giving:
Encourage Life in the Decay

*When trees die, the world springs
anew—if you let it.*

The volatile heart of Mount St. Helens sits imprisoned on my desk, her ashes tiny remnants of the day she spilled her guts to the world.

On that morning in May 1980, trees came crashing down in 150 square miles of forest around the volcano's blast zone, and ashen dust blackened skies as far away as Spokane before circling the earth. As soon as the air cleared around his Portland home to the south, my grandfather went outside, scooped from his gutter the tiny pieces of that old volcano who could no longer contain herself, bottled them up in a glass pharmaceutical jar, and saved them for me.

In the thirty-six years since then, the fine gray powder has stayed as inert and lifeless as scientists predicted the mountain itself would be for years to come. There had to be few survivors, they'd surmised during the hours after the eruption, and those who did manage to crawl out of the ash and pumice would likely find nothing to live on.

But nature had other ideas, defying much of what scientists knew—or thought they knew—about the potential for regeneration in the veritable moonscape. US Forest Service research ecologist

Gophers were nature's gardeners in the aftermath
of the Mount St. Helens eruption, pushing
soil up onto the ashen landscape and creating
new habitat for plants and other animals.

Charlie Crisafulli remembers the startling contrast with the majestic old-growth trees and sparkling lakes he saw from a helicopter en route to the blast site. "You come out into this vast terrain of steaming gray, and when you set the chopper down, big plumes of dust come up. And you're walking, and you're sinking into the ash, and it's being kicked up everywhere. It's so dramatically different from what it had been, and it's so harsh, and it seems so extreme, [you think] how could anything have survived?"

In the weeks and months ahead, though, Crisafulli and his colleagues would spot hundreds, then thousands, of plants pushing up through the lifeless-looking landscape. They would be stunned to see how quickly surviving gophers proliferated, serving as gardeners in the barren landscape by mixing nutrient-poor volcanic deposits with the rich soil buried below. They would watch in fascination as those gopher burrows collapsed under the feet of returning elk, creating tiny havens for amphibians who needed an escape from the summer heat. They would find fish in new pools formed by fallen trees in blast zone streams. They would see death giving way to life, as birds nested and foraged in tree snags and fungi colonized scorched wood that released nutrients back into the wounded earth.

It took an act of Congress to protect the land now known as Mount St. Helens National Volcanic Monument, a 110,000-acre living laboratory for scientists studying nature's response to natural cataclysm. The timber industry and the federal government moved into the other areas, removing dead wood and planting new trees. Unlike the monument's natural patchwork of emerging habitats, these man-made monocultures are much less diverse, supporting far fewer bird and small mammal species. Without the understory found in naturally evolving forests, the trees stand tall and straight, but they stand largely alone.

In describing the eruption's magnitude, some sources refer to the number of trees in "board feet," a timber industry term in use since at least the decades when my ancestors were logging in the Pacific Northwest. In late 1919 and early 1920, my great-grandfather, in a contract with the federal government, took about twelve and a half million board feet of spruce logs over the course of four months. By comparison, Mount St. Helens blew down more than four billion board feet in one morning.

Though on different time scales, both the forces of nature and the forces of the timber industry scrape the land. But as ecologists have learned, there's a critical difference in what is left behind. The volcano may have scrubbed the area nearly raw in one terrible, cataclysmic swoop, but the plants have been allowed to grow back, to reorganize themselves from vestiges of roots, rhizomes, and seeds—and to be joined by countless organisms arriving by wind and water or their own legs and wings. It won't ever be the same again, but its new incarnation is unexpectedly beautiful and, scientists say, even more diverse than before.

Commercial logging has been built on the idea of razing the land, as has the commercialization of our home landscapes. The disturbance on most of our properties has been far less abrupt, at least in areas like mine, where eastern broadleaf deciduous forest gave way to agriculture and then to dense human habitation over the course of centuries. But what the destruction in the name of turfgrass monocultures lacks in suddenness, it makes up for in frequency; instead of one devastating blast, we create death by a thousand cuts with our

Cleaning up some leaves around the patio one spring, I found a colorful caterpillar, possibly on his way to finding a place to pupate. If I'd been using a leaf blower or raked the leaves into bags, he likely would never have become a mourning cloak butterfly.

string trimmers and leaf blowers and power mowers, cutting up caterpillars in the violets and raking up beetles in the leaves week after week and year after year.

Debates over the merits of creating backyard habitat sometimes take a detour to belligerent diatribes about the impossibility of restoring nature to some previously pristine state. Such discussions are an unfortunate distraction. By observing how natural landscapes evolve, we can build on still viable vestiges of disturbed ecologies—what Crisafulli refers to as the memory in the land—to create new habitat where much has been lost.

Life after death

Sometimes those losses are harder to discern, as Gillian Martin discovered when she began hearing similar versions of the same tale over and over again from local bluebird advocates. On the face of it, the story was enchanting: A woman arrives at a local park in early spring and opens the trunk of her car to retrieve the nest box she has refurbished just in time for the new season. Soon she notices a bluebird pair eyeing her. As she walks across the grass, box in hand, the birds follow her. So eager to start their family, they even land on the box before it's fully secured in a tree.

Though an old birdhouse in our yard violates many building codes set by bluebird societies, this family found it anyway and raised two generations—probably because they have few other options in a community where too many dead trees are still removed.

If it had happened only once, maybe Martin could have written it off as a fluke. But as she sat in the meetings of the Southern California Bluebird Club and heard it echoed repeatedly, she realized something was amiss.

"Every time that story was told, the siren in my head got louder," Martin says. The boxes were creating dependence on humans, she realized, and artificially supporting a population that couldn't find enough natural habitat to survive on its own.

North America's three bluebird species are secondary cavity nesters, relying on existing tree holes or those carved out by woodpeckers and other animals. In the distant past, tree snags and old wooden fence posts provided plenty such habitats, but by the twentieth century, development and clear-cutting put bluebirds on the path to extinction. Pesticides and competition for nesting sites from introduced species exacerbated their plight.

With the help of citizen activists who built and monitored nest boxes, bluebirds staged a comeback—in some places spectacularly so. But though valuable, nest boxes are a Band-Aid solution to a wounded landscape, with sometimes unintended consequences: in western Montana, researchers recently found that their prevalence has created an imbalance, enabling western bluebirds to outcompete mountain bluebirds in a territory they'd been cohabiting for thousands of years.[1]

Addressing the problem at its source, Martin concluded, is the only sustainable answer, and in 2012, that realization drove her to found the Cavity Conservation Initiative under the auspices of the bluebird club. Now known in the county as the "snag lady," Martin has worked the system from every angle, promoting the value of dead and dying trees to county park administrators, rangers, school officials, golf course managers, and the tree care industry. She has forged alliances with government and nonprofit entities and recently submitted a proposal to incorporate tree snag preservation in a federal urban park initiative.

She's not doing it just for the bluebirds. At least eighty-five species of birds in North America are cavity-nesters, and dead trees—often referred to as "wildlife trees"—sustain countless other organisms. As bacteria and fungi move in to hasten the decay of snags, stumps, and fallen logs, beetles tunnel through the softening wood to lay their eggs, followed by wood-nesting native bees. Nature's homebuilders, the woodpeckers, show up to eat the insects and nest. In ensuing years their handiwork creates condos for swallows, squirrels, and owls. Raccoons, martens, porcupines, foxes, bobcats, and even bears take refuge in snags and hollowed-out logs. Owls and hawks perch on top to survey their domains. Acorn woodpeckers make a kitchen pantry out of dying trees, caching their food there.

Humans also use dead wood—to frame our homes, support our beds, and hold the plates we eat from. Is it any wonder that the animals need dead and dying trees, not to mention all their shed leaves, for much the same reasons? But unlike the vibrant bluebird, the quiet, life-giving beauty of plants past their prime does not easily sell itself. Too often thought of as mere fire hazards, insect hosts, and disease spreaders, these backbones of nature have been chopped down, raked, and carried out like trash from forests and our home landscapes. "When we haul away a tree needlessly, we take away half its life's destiny," says Martin. "If trees could speak to us when we're doing that, they would scream at us."

Vestiges of the forest can sustain life long after their dying day, as many organisms move in to feed on the decay. On a fallen tree in my yard, witches' butter fungus appears after rains. As the grubs of other beetle species move in to feed on the rotting wood, predatory eastern-eyed click beetle larvae move in to eat the grubs. The nectar-eating adults are acrobats, flipping themselves upside down into the air while making a clicking sound when threatened.

A Nuttall's woodpecker feeds his young in a tree cavity in Irvine, California. The species also nests in dead branches on live trees and stumps as short as two to three feet.

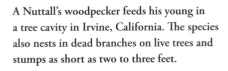

Brown creepers forage and roost in loosening pockets of bark.

With a few of the following simple modifications, gardeners on properties large and small can integrate dying trees and fallen leaves in their landscapes.

Turn a wildlife tree into a centerpiece.

As she watches real-life creatures congregate on dying oaks and sycamores near her Virginia home, landscape designer Mary Sper sees fantastical representations of antelopes and other creatures, finding shapes in the branch structure the way some might imagine them in clouds. "I tend to notice them more than the living trees around them," she says.

In the garden, a tree snag can be a free sculptural asset, she says. Blend one into the landscape by training Virginia creeper or another native vine to climb it. Provide shelter and a feeling of safety for cautious songbirds by surrounding the snag with serviceberries, redbuds, fruiting shrubs, or other understory species helpful to wildlife in your region. By making the snag a purposeful part of the habitat garden, Sper notes, you may also satisfy skeptical human neighbors.

When considering keeping a snag near a house or walkway, consult a trained tree-care professional to be sure it's still securely rooted and safe.

Make log houses for earth dwellers.

Even if you have to remove a tree, Nuttall's woodpeckers, a California species, will nest in stumps as low as two to three feet off the ground, says Martin. In my yard on the East Coast, pileated woodpeckers still feast on the foot-tall remains of invasive Siberian elms we cut down ten years ago. Logs and cut branches lining beds or placed throughout

Tree snags, stumps, and logs can be one-of-a-kind sculptural assets in a garden.

Logs, rocks, bark, and other debris provide lifelong homes to red-backed salamanders, who are born in clusters in these hidden places and hunt for insects, spiders, earthworms, centipedes, and other invertebrates. Mother salamanders guard their eggs by coiling around them for weeks until they hatch.

Woolly bears, the caterpillars of Isabella tiger moths, are among many creatures who produce an antifreeze-like substance to survive the winter under leaves.

the garden nurture salamanders and other species. Even dead limbs on live trees can provide nesting sites; leave them in place if they pose no dangers.

Turtles, birds, and many other animals can find shelter and insects in brush piles made from branches and twigs. Depending on your tastes and your neighborhood's landscaping standards, you can arrange them neatly, let them develop more naturally, or add them to areas hidden from public view.

Let leaves blanket your gardens.

Without their chlorophyll, leaves may appear to the uninitiated to have lost their relevance. But as they decompose, they'll add structure and nutrients to the soil, nurture new plant growth, and feed the many creatures whose lives begin in the decay. A square meter of soil can contain more than a trillion microbes working hard to decompose organic remains and make essential nutrients available to plant roots. Alongside them is a diverse community of larger predators and recyclers—including springtails, mites, millipedes, snails, earwigs, crickets, beetles, and worms—who together make a rich banquet for toads, birds, and other foragers.

Leaves fallen from sumacs provide a place for red-banded hairstreak butterflies to lay their eggs, and rich leaf litter gives ovenbirds the material they need for their oven-shaped nests. Protect these creatures by leaving the leaves where you can or, if you must remove them from an area, placing them under trees and shrubs and around existing gardens. Avoid using leaf blowers, which can be catastrophic, ripping like tornados through habitat and removing essential shelter and food.

Newspaper topped with leaves, mulch, and garden debris kills grass naturally, protecting the soil community underneath while making way for new gardens to be enjoyed by descendants of this pearl crescent butterfly and many other creatures. Sometimes called "lasagna gardening," this method is an animal-friendly alternative to using chemicals or heavy equipment to prepare new beds.

In milkweed pods and other remains of the season, we can find seeds of renewal.

Don't deadhead; "live-head" instead.

Retail marketers and popular gardening magazines still encourage "spring cleanup" and "winterizing" of the garden through pruning of branches and deadheading (or removal) of spent flowers. But seed heads sustain animals through the lean season and well into spring, so consider leaving a patch standing all year. If you need to remove them from more visible areas, try waiting until late spring and proceed carefully: bees might still be nesting in the pithy stems, but you can protect these larvae by breaking the stalks into foot-long pieces and scattering them under shrubs.

Our misunderstanding of death and decay has led to some startling phenomena: front lawns made of plastic turf, deserts sprinkled with water-guzzling golf courses, developments filled with palm trees and invasive plants out of sync with their surroundings. But instead of deifying the color green, a humane gardener appreciates the land and all its iterations and hues through every season. In winter, even though it feels like nature is retreating, it's still there. The birds' struggle to find seeds and insects becomes our struggle. The deer lying under the brush and quietly grooming her front paws isn't that different from our dogs who do the same on a rug indoors—or from us, for that matter. We all need a safe space and a little sustenance to get us through the day.

By taking advantage of the opportunity to view the world as it goes dormant, we can observe without distraction the bones of our surroundings. Shedding their extravagant petticoats of summer, the trees reveal the structure of their limbs, and we see through them. Letting go of their rough exteriors, the milkweed pods and goldenrod seed heads spill out fluffy promises. In them we remember the shapes of things past and, if we take the time to view the world from other species' perspectives, envision the bounty of all that is to come.

Portland landscape designer Eileen Stark may never know what plants and creatures once lived where her home now stands, but that doesn't matter to the hummingbirds, varied thrushes, and western tanagers who stop by to nest and forage. The lot is large for a city yard but small by most other standards, yet it has a depth of vegetation and decay that brings birds typically only seen in a forest. More of a land in transition than a land in recovery, it's designed around animals' needs, providing a quiet area in the back where they can forage and rest in peace, away from human presence. In honoring the lives of the trees and of the bees who take refuge in their shedding leaves, this garden made by human hands is allowed to grow and decay at nature's pace, slowly enough to harbor the seeds and cocoons of rebirth.

Eileen Stark

landscape designer

*An urban woodland and pollinator garden
in Portland, Oregon*

The day was unusually warm for early spring, a fine time in Eileen Stark's mind to do a little digging in the garden. But the queen bee taking cover there wasn't so keen on the idea. "She was still hibernating," says Stark, who accidentally evicted her. "I felt so bad. She was under a lot of leaf litter."

Relieved when the bee soon returned home to snuggle under the leaves again, Stark put a kind of "do not disturb" sign around the area—a few well-placed rocks to remind herself of the presence of a hardworking mom getting in some last winks before emerging to start a new bumblebee colony.

To reduce the chances of another unearthing, Stark now avoids digging in early spring and late fall. "Even when you're being careful, you can accidentally disturb a nest if you don't know where it is," she says.

Thanks to a pair of binoculars and a bird guide her parents kept by the windowsill, "I could name a lot of birds by the time I was five," says Stark. Between earning her landscaping design degree and starting her company, Second Nature Garden Design, she spent nine years channeling her affinity for animals into an advocacy career dedicated to the passage of stronger animal cruelty laws.

But while the work to address roadside zoos, factory farms, and other exploitive industries is essential, the focus on animals elsewhere sometimes overshadows the needs of creatures living right among us. "We think about animals that are in captivity, and of course we should," she says, "but we don't think about what we're doing to animals right outside our back door."

For Stark, each step into her outdoor space is guided by a principle that the animals come first, even when their webbing blocks her path. As a child, Stark learned from her mother not to fear spiders but to bring them outside. Since then, she has come to admire their graceful movement, their sensitivity to vibrations and airflow, their decision-making powers, and the protectiveness some species show toward their young. She appreciates their role as predator, prey, and provider; their webs provide insects for hummingbirds, and Stark has seen chickadee parents gather spiders for their babies. Most of all, she admires their patience, a quality she tries to show them in return. Rather than expecting these often maligned creatures to move aside for her, Stark changes course to let the webs be when possible. "Or I'll try to limbo under them and kill my back."

As a professional in the horticulture industry, Stark helps clients bring outdoor spaces alive through lush, ecological plantings. But as a wildlife advocate, she knows there is just as much life in fallen leaves and other seemingly dead spaces—decaying logs, rock piles, and leftover perennial stalks. "Piles of logs—especially when they get a little older and moss-covered—I think they're really beautiful. In a shady garden, they're just lovely interspersed among the plants," she says. "I always recommend people do that and make them big enough—not just a couple of little branches but a good little pile—for a bird who wants to get out of the rain or escape from a predator, or for a little mouse."

Though Stark is the author of *Real Gardens Grow Natives*, she prefers a phase-in approach toward native plants, adding them whenever possible while leaving in place nonnative plants used by wildlife

Hummingbirds use materials including lichen and spiderwebs to camouflage their delicate nests from predators. Stark had a rare opportunity to watch these babies grow when their mother chose to raise them in a rhododendron near a window.

Cedar waxwings visit the garden during fall migration, showing up by the hundreds to devour figs and native berries, including this Cascade Oregon grape.

Varied thrushes began appearing in Stark's yard after she turned parts of it into a miniwoodland with layers of decaying leaves. These shy denizens of Pacific Northwest forests forage on the ground and in low shrubs and trees.

This western red cedar had already reached thirty feet only twelve years after Stark planted it. It's one of her favorite species in the yard because of the sustenance it provides insects and birds and the thermal cover of its branches.

and posing no invasive threats. "In a perfect world, we'd be growing mostly natives—I think the more we can grow, the better," she says. "But that's not always possible. If there's a huge tree in your backyard and it's attracting lots of birds and bees and lots of insects, there's no reason to take that out if it's not native, because you're doing a lot of damage to the wildlife that was using it."

Animals have validated this "first, do no harm" philosophy. Apple and apricot trees planted near the driveway draw hungry squirrels. Cedar waxwings descend on the garden during fall migration, devouring the Asian figs that came with the house. One summer a mama hummingbird found just the right spot to build her nest in a large exotic rhododendron planted by previous homeowners, feeding periodically on the native red-flowering currants Stark had planted nearby.

A neighbor's removal of a large ponderosa pine that had been home to many nesting birds—all because he didn't like the way the tree shed needles—gave Stark extra impetus to provide even more habitat. A western red cedar she planted twelve years ago now stands thirty feet tall. At the far end of the backyard, under the shade of the cedar and Douglas fir, is a quiet area created to minimize disturbance and human activity. "Most wildlife—with exceptions like hummingbirds and chickadees—really don't like our presence and want to be left alone, and they like quiet," says Stark. "I think we have to just kind of mimic nature. Think: How would nature do this?"

Tiny creatures taking shelter on the ground feed larger species of the sky. Varied thrushes swoop in to explore decaying leaves for insects and slugs, looking, as Stark says, as if they'd forgotten where they put their keys. Her affection for the birds is magnified by their vulnerability: the species declined in population by more than 75 percent between 1966 and 2014, according to the North American Breeding Bird Survey. In fact, the sound of their ethereal calls on hikes used to be Stark's only exposure to them. "Before we bought our house and turned a lot of the yard into basically shady areas with a lot of leaves, I'd never really seen one before," she says.

Throughout the yard, birds forage and perch on brush piles anchored by crisscrossed logs. Clustered roses, Oregon grapes, snowberry, California hazelnut, and redtwig dogwood beckon animals with their fruit and flowers. Ferns, foamflower, inside-out flower, wild ginger, bunchberry, goatsbeard, bugbane, trillium, Hooker's fairybells, and other perennials of varying heights blanket the understory. Further toward the house are quaking aspens, blueberries, strawberries, serviceberries, thimbleberries, nodding onions, penstemon, beach daisy, and a vegetable garden.

Stark is trying to grow a Pacific madrone tree for the third time, after installing it next to an exotic magnolia slated for removal. Attractive to many species, from bees and azure butterflies to nesting birds to elk, the madrone is sensitive to overwatering and adjusts its habits to sun and surroundings, twisting and turning its red bark in rockier places to finally reach the light. After a successful first year, Stark thinks this time her new madrone may just survive, growing straight and tall to spread its white-flowering and orange-berrying branches far and wide—a feast for the eyes of humans and bellies of animals seeking safety in the urban refuge.

Getting Started

Humane Gardener

www.humanegardener.com

The Humane Gardener website provides more information on the concepts explored in this book. Through blogs, interviews, species profiles, and tips from wildlife gardeners, readers can learn how to convert traditional landscapes into welcoming spaces for all species.

The Natural Web

www.the-natural-web.org

Exploring nature's connections, with beautiful photos of plants, animals, and other organisms, this blog by naturalist Mary Anne Borge helps readers learn more about interactions among species they might find in their own gardens.

EcoBeneficial

www.ecobeneficial.com

Filled with informative Q&As, videos, how-tos, and book reviews, EcoBeneficial, founded by horticulturist Kim Eierman, provides information on the latest research in ecological gardening and tips for how to apply best practices in the home landscape.

Regional Books on Habitat Gardening

The websites of many state native plant societies and natural resource agencies provide recommended reading lists for gardeners. The following books represent a sampling of these regional guides. Some tips in certain books are not in line with my own recommendations; for example, there is an overwhelming tendency to divide backyard visitors into "desirable" and "undesirable" wildlife. But they all contain helpful advice about local plant selection and the habitat needs of many wild visitors.

PACIFIC NORTHWEST

Real Gardens Grow Natives
Design, Plant and Enjoy a Healthy Northwest Garden
by Eileen Stark (2014)

SOUTHWEST

Texas Wildscapes
Gardening for Wildlife
by Kelly Conrad Bender (2009)

MIDWEST

The Midwestern Native Garden
by Charlotte Adelman and Bernard L. Schwartz (2011)

SOUTHEAST

Native Plant Landscaping for Florida Wildlife
by Craig N. Huegel (2010)

NORTHEAST

The Green Garden
A New England Guide to Planting and Maintaining the Eco-Friendly Habitat Garden
by Ellen Sousa (2011)

MID-ATLANTIC

Chesapeake Gardening & Landscaping
The Essential Green Guide
by Barbara W. Ellis (2015)

Native Plants for Wildlife Habitat and Conservation Landscaping
Chesapeake Bay Watershed
by US Fish and Wildlife Service (2005)
www.nativeplantcenter.net

Native Plant Information and Regional Databases

Native Plant Information Network

Lady Bird Johnson Wildflower Center

www.wildflower.org/plants

NPIN offers the most comprehensive database of plants native to the United States and Canada. Searching by scientific or common name, gardeners can access detailed fact sheets about a plant's natural habitat, distribution, soil and light needs, and benefits to wildlife. The site also allows visitors to create lists of species native to their states or provinces and suitable to the conditions of their own gardens.

Native Plants Finder

National Wildlife Federation

www.nwf.org/NativePlantFinder/

This new online tool, developed by the National Wildlife Federation in partnership with the University of Delaware and the US Forest Service, provides lists of plants most helpful to wildlife. Searchable by zip code, the database prioritizes local natives that attract a high number of butterfly and moth caterpillars, a mainstay of baby bird diets.

Ecoregional Planting Guides

Pollinator Partnership

www.pollinator.org/guides.htm

From prairie to desert to mountainous regions, these thirty-two downloadable guides cover a diversity of habitats across North America. Explaining how pollinators rely on flower color and shape, the guides also provide information about nesting needs and region-specific plant lists.

National Suppliers Directory

Lady Bird Johnson Wildflower Center

www.wildflower.org/suppliers

Up-to-date listings of native plant nurseries, seed companies, and landscape professionals are searchable by city, state, and zip code.

Native Plant Society Listings

North American Native Plant Society

www.nanps.org/index.php/resources/native-plant-societies

The NANPS, based in Toronto, provides links to state and provincial native plant societies. Many of these regional and local sites offer a wealth of information about native plant nurseries and upcoming native plant sales and events.

Coexisting with Wildlife

Wild Neighbors

Humane Society of the United States

www.humanesociety.org/wildneighbors

The HSUS website and book, *Wild Neighbors: The Humane Approach to Living with Wildlife* (Washington, DC: Humane Society of the United States, 2007), offer comprehensive information about excluding wild animals from homes and other structures, helping orphaned and injured wildlife, and vetting wildlife-control operators to avoid hiring a disreputable service.

The Wildlife-Friendly Vegetable Gardener
How to Grow Food in Harmony with Nature
by Tammi Hartung (2014)

This book is a one-of-a-kind guide to growing food for all species, including our own and any other visitors to our backyards.

Habitat Certification and Yard Signs

You can let neighbors know what you're up to—and perhaps even recruit some new wildlife gardeners—by posting an official habitat sign in your front yard. Many native plant societies, state and local environmental agencies, national wildlife protection organizations, and pollinator-conservation initiatives offer habitat certification of home gardens. Here are a few favorites:

Certified Wildlife Habitat Program
National Wildlife Federation
www.nwf.org/wildlifehabitat

Pollinator Habitat program
The Xerces Society for Invertebrate Conservation
www.xerces.org/pollinatorhabitat

Humane Backyard
Humane Society of the United States
www.humanesociety.org/humanebackyard

#SavetheBats
Organization for Bat Conservation
www.batconservation.org/help/bat-gardens

Monarch Waystation Program
MonarchWatch
www.monarchwatch.org/waystations

Cavity Conservation Initiative
cavityconservation.com/nature-store-2/

The initiative's "Wildlife Tree" sign provides a brief explanation of why you've chosen to let a dead tree remain standing.

Plants Mentioned in This Book

For ease of reading, scientific names appear here next to common names of species highlighted in the narrative. Though cumbersome, Latin nomenclature is more foolproof, since a single species sometimes goes by multiple common names, and a single common name is sometimes accorded to multiple species. Adding to the taxonomical confusion are new methods of genetic analysis that have upended centuries-old plant classifications. Most of the plants we still call "asters," for example, are no longer in the *Aster* genus; where I've noted in the book that asters feed caterpillars of pearl crescent butterflies and brown-hooded owlet moths, I'm really referring to plants in the genus now known scientifically as *Symphyotrichum*.

When a native species is mentioned in the context of a specific garden or region, the Latin name for that species is provided; the first word indicates the genus to which the species belongs. In the case of general references to a group of plants, only the genus is listed, followed by the abbreviation for species ("spp")—indicating a reference to more than one native species within the group.

Knowing the genus can help you determine if similar plants grow in your own region; for example, the bunchberry (*Cornus unalaschkensis*) mentioned in Chapter 6 is native only to western Canada and the American West Coast, but another bunchberry (*Cornus canadensis*) is native to the northern United States, Colorado, New Mexico, and Canada.

Because this continent spans a diverse range of climates and terrains, plants adapted to the local ecology of one area may be inappropriate for another. And non-native plants considered weeds, such as plantains, often have lesser-known American counterparts, like *Plantago rugelii*, a native inhabitant of disturbed sites.

Native Species

spp. indicates a reference to more than one native species within the group

var. indicates the taxonomic rank "variety," which is below species and subspecies

American beautyberry
Callicarpa americana

American hazelnut
Corylus americana

Anise hyssop
Agastache foeniculum

Aster
Symphyotrichum spp.

Bayberry
Myrica pensylvanica

Beach daisy
Erigeron glaucus

Bee balm
Monarda didyma

Blackberry
Rubus spp.

Black cherry
Prunus serotina

Black locust
Robinia pseudoacacia

Black raspberry
Rubus occidentalis

Black walnut
Juglans nigra

Blueberry
Vaccinium spp.

Blue false indigo
Baptisia australis

Blue mistflower
Conoclinium coelestinum

Blue vervain
Verbena hastata

Boneset
Eupatorium serotinum or *Eupatorium perfoliatum*

Broomsedge
Andropogon virginicus

Buckwheat
Eriogonum spp.

Bunchberry
Cornus unalaschkensis

Bush's coneflower
Echinacea paradoxa

California fuschia
Epilobium canum

California hazelnut
Corylus cornuta var. *californica*

California poppy
Eschscholzia californica

Cardinal flower
Lobelia cardinalis

Carolina allspice
Calycanthus floridus

Chalk dudleya
Dudleya pulverulenta

Chocolate flower
Berlandiera lyrata

Chokeberry
Photinia melanocarpa

Cleveland sage
Salvia clevelandii

Clustered rose
Rosa pisocarpa

Columbine
Aquilegia spp.

Common evening primrose
Oenothera biennis

Common milkweed
Asclepias tuberosa

Coral honeysuckle
Lonicera sempervirens

Cowslip
Heracleum maximum

Crabapple
Malus coronaria

Cudweed
Gamochaeta spp.

Cup plant
Silphium perfoliatum

Cutleaf coneflower
Rudbeckia laciniata

Cypress
Taxodium distichum

Dense blazing star
Liatris spicata

Dogbane
Apocynum cannibinum

Dogwood
Cornus spp.

Douglas fir
Pseudotsuga menziesii

Eastern red cedar
Juniperus virginiana

Elderberry
Sambucus nigra spp. *canadensis; Sambucus racemosa*

False sunflower
Heliopsis helianthoides

Fireweed
Chamerion angustifolium

Foamflower
Tiarella trifoliata var. *trifoliate*

Forked aster
Eurybia furcata

Fringe tree
Chionanthus virginicus

Fuschia-flowering gooseberry
Ribes speciosum

Goatsbeard
Aruncus dioicus

Golden alexander
Zizia aurea

Golden ragwort
Packera aurea

Goldenrod
Solidago spp.

Grapevine
Vitis spp.

Gray dogwood
Cornus racemosa
Heath aster
Symphytrichum ericoides
Hickory
Carya spp.
Hoaryleaf ceanothus
Ceanothus crassifolius
Holly
Ilex spp.
Hollyleaf redberry
Rhamnus ilicifolia
Hooker's fairybells
Prosartes hookeri
Indiangrass
Sorghastrum nutans
Inside-out flower
Vancouveria hexandra
Jewelweed
Impatiens capensis
Joe-pye weed
Eutrochium spp.
Leafless beaked orchid
Stenorrhynchos lanceolatum
Liatris
Liatris spp.
Little bluestem
Schizachyrium scoparium
Longleaf pine
Pinus palustris
Mayapple
Podophyllum peltatum
Milkweed
Asclepias spp.

Mission manzanita
Xylococcus bicolor
Monkeyflower
Mimulus spp.
Nodding onion
Allium cernuum
Oak
Quercus spp.
Oregon grape (Cascade; tall)
Mahonia nervosa; Mahonia aquifolium
Pacific madrone
Arbutus menziesii
Parlin's pussytoes
Antennaria parlinii
Passionflower
Passiflora incarnata
Pawpaw
Asimina triloba
Pearly Everlasting
Anaphalis margaritacea
Penstemon
Penstemon spp. (also called beardtongue)
Pine lily
Lilium catesbaei
Plainleaf pussytoes
Antennaria plantaginifolia
Plantain
Plantago spp.
Pokeweed
Phytolacca americana
Ponderosa pine
Pinus ponderosa

Possumhaw viburnum
Viburnum nudum
Prairie dropseed
Sporobolus heterolepis
Prairie phlox
Phlox pilosa
Prickly pear
Opuntia humifusa
Purple coneflower
Echinacea purpurea
Purple lovegrass
Eragrostis spectabilis
Purple prairie clover
Dalea purpurea
Quaking aspen
Populus tremuloides
Queen-of-the-prairie
Filipendula rubra
Rabbitbells
Crotalaria rotundifolia
Raspberry
Rubus spp.
Redbud
Cercis canadensis
Redbush monkeyflower
Mimulus aurantiacus var. *puniceus*
Redtwig dogwood
Cornus sericea
River oats
Chasmanthum latifolium
Rose
Rosa spp.
Sage
Salvia spp.

Sagebrush
Artemisia spp.
San Diego mountain
mahogany
*Cercocarpus
minutiflorus*
Sassafras
Sassafras albidum
Serviceberry
Amelanchier spp.
Showy penstemon
Penstemon spectabilis
Shrubby St. John's wort
Hypericum prolificum
Skullcap
Scutellaria lateriflora
Snowberry
Symphoricarpos albus
Southern honeysuckle
Lonicera subspicata
Spanish needles
Bidens alba
Spicebush
Lindera benzoin
Staghorn sumac
Rhus typhina
Strawberry
Fragaria spp.
Sugar maple
Acer saccharum
Sumac
Rhus spp.
Sunflower
Helianthus spp.
Swamp milkweed
Asclepias incarnata

Switchgrass
Panicum virgatum
Tall bugbane
Actaea elata
Thimbleberry
Rubus parviflorus
Trillium
Trillium ovatum
Turk's cap lily
Lilium superbum
Viburnum
Viburnum spp.
Violet
Viola sororia and
other native *Viola*
spp.
Virginia bluebells
Mertensia virginiana
Virginia creeper
*Parthenocissus
quinequefolia*
Virginia rose
Rosa virginiana
Washington hawthorn
*Crataegus
phaenopyrum*
Wax myrtle
Myrica cerifera
Western red cedar
Thuja plicata
White avens
Geum canadense
White sage
Salvia apiana
Wild bergamot
Monarda fistulosa

Wild ginger
Asarum caudatum
Willow
Salix spp.
Winterberry holly
Ilex verticillata
Woodland phlox
Phlox divaricata
Yellow bush penstemon
*Keckiella
antirrhinoides*
Yucca
Yucca spp.

Some nonnative species that were introduced centuries ago are helpful to wildlife; dandelions, for example, sustain spring pollinators and feed bears, greater prairie chickens, sage grouse, rabbits, and deer. Even so, it's best to plant and encourage natives whenever possible, since many plants introduced outside their natural ranges—including a few on this list—were thought to be tame garden plants until they escaped cultivation and began invading habitat.

Nonnative Species

* indicates invasive status in one or more state or province

x indicates the plant is a hybrid

Apple
Malus domestica

Apricot
Prunus armeniaca

Bindweed
Convolvulus arvensis*

Burning bush
Euonymus alatus*

Curry plant
Helichrysum italicum

Dame's rocket
Hesperis matronalis*

Dandelion
Taraxacum officinale

Daylily
Hemerocallis spp.*

English ivy
Hedera helix*

European buckthorn
Rhamnus cathartica*

Fennel
Foeniculum vulgare

Fig
Ficus carica

Forsythia
Forsythia spp.

Garlic mustard
Alliaria petiolata*

Gingko
Gingko biloba

Hollyhock
Alcea rosea

Licorice plant
Helichrysum petiolare

Lilac
Syringa vulgaris

Linden
Tilia tomentosa and *Tilia cordata*

Japanese barberry
Berberis thungbergii*

Japanese honeysuckle
Lonicera japonica*

Nandina
Nandina domestica*

Norway maples
Acer platanoides*

Parsley
Petroselinum crispum

Peppermint
Mentha x *piperita*

Purple deadnettle
Lamium purpureum*

Queen Anne's lace
Daucus carota*

Rhododendron
Rhododendron spp.
(Though often over-looked in favor of cultivated Asian varieties, dozens of rhododendron species are native to the United States.)

Rue
Ruta graveolens

Savory
Satureja hortensis and *Satureja montana*

Siberian elm
Ulmus pumila*

Strawberry
Fragaria spp.

Tuberous begonias
Begonia x *tuberhybrida*

Zinnia
Zinnia elegans

Notes

INTRODUCTION

1 See "How to Use Bayer Advanced Insect Killer for Optimum Lawn Pest Control—The Home Depot," YouTube video, 2:00, posted by Home Depot, March 8, 2012, https://www.youtube.com/watch?v=KvPuWQ3bDj0; "5 Reasons Why You Should Remove Dead Trees," Ron's Tree Service and Firewood, July 15, 2015, http://www.ronstreeserviceandfirewood.com/5-reasons-why-you-should-remove-dead-trees; and "Groundhog Control & Removal," Nationwide Wildlife Removal-2016, http://www.aaanimalcontrol.com/professional-trapper/howtogetridofgroundhogs.htm.

2 See North American Bird Conservation Initiative. *The State of North America's Birds 2016* (Ottawa, Ont.: Environment and Climate Change, 2016). Canada: Ottawa, Ontario. 8 pages. http://www.stateofthebirds.org/2016/; World Wildlife Fund [R. McLellan, L. Iyengar, B. Jeffries, and N. Oerlemans, eds.], *Living Planet Report 2014: Species and spaces, people and places* (Gland, Switzerland: World Wildlife Fund), http://assets.worldwildlife.org/publications/723/files/original/WWF-LPR2014-low_res.pdf; and Intergovernmental Science-Policy Platform on Biodiversity and Ecosystem Services (IPBES), "Deliverable 3(a): Thematic assessment of pollinators, pollination and food production," ipbes.net/work-programme/pollination.

3 See C. Milesi et al., "A Strategy for Mapping and Modeling the Ecological Effects of US Lawns," Joint Symposia URBAN-URS (2005), International Society for Photogrammetry and Remote Sensing, http://www.isprs.org/proceedings/XXXVI/8-W27/milesi.pdf. The Environmental Protection Agency's most recent market report estimates use of conventional pesticides in lawn, garden, and home applications at nearly 70 million pounds; see "Pesticides Industry Sales and Usage: 2006-2007 Market Estimates," https://www.epa.gov/sites/production/files/2015-10/documents/market_estimates2007.pdf. At the time of writing, the EPA expected to release a new report by the fall of 2016.

CHAPTER 1

1 This estimate was calculated by entomologist Doug Tallamy, based on the percentage of species introduced by the horticultural trade and profiled in Sylvan Ramsey Kaufman and Wallace Kaufman, *Invasive Plants: Guide*

to Identification and the Impacts and Control of Common North American Species (Mechanicsburg, PA: Stackpole Books, 2012).

2 A growing body of research supports the notion of nature as critical to our well-being. Two excellent resources are Richard Louv, *The Nature Principle: Reconnecting with Life in a Virtual Age* (Chapel Hill: Algonquin Books, 2012), and articles posted by the American Society of Landscape Architects, asla.org/healthbenefitsofnature.aspx.

3 Some researchers contend that East Coast monarchs aren't suffering from a loss of milkweed as much as from a dearth of fall wildflowers that provide nectar on their migration back to Mexico. See Hidetoshi Inamine, Stephen P. Ellner, James P. Springer, and Anurag A. Agrawal, "Linking the continental migratory cycle of the monarch butterfly to understand its population decline," *Oikos* (April 27, 2016).

4 Scientists have found surprising evidence of the coevolution of flower shapes and bee tongues. As drier weather caused by climate change decreased populations of their preferred plants in the Rocky Mountains, two bumblebee species were forced to forage from a greater diversity of flowers—and their tongue lengths shortened considerably over the course of only four decades. See N. E. Miller-Struttmann et al., "Functional mismatch in a bumble bee population mutualism under climate change," *Science* (September 25, 2015).

5 Most ecological landscape designers and gardeners recommend clearing an area of invasives prior to planting. But the idea of inserting natives directly into patches of invasive plants is described in a case study of a New Jersey gardener in Claudia West and Thomas Rainer, *Planting in a Post-Wild World* (Portland: Timber Press, 2015). A similar method pioneered in natural areas by two Australian sisters is described in Jean Walker and Joan Bradley, *Bringing Back the Bush: The Bradley Method of Bush Regeneration* (Chatswood, NSW: New Holland Publishing Australia, 2002).

6 Research by University of Vermont PhD student Annie White shows that bees strongly prefer the flowers of straight native species in some cases but are just as attracted to cultivars in others. "One clear trend was observed," she writes. "The more manipulated the cultivars became, the less attractive they became to pollinators"; see "From Nursery to Nature: Are native cultivars as valuable to pollinators as native species?," posted February 8, 2013, updated March 1, 2016, https://pollinatorgardens.org/2013/02/08/my-research/). Similarly, studies by Tallamy and the Mt. Cuba Center in Delaware are demonstrating a range of results: elms and chestnuts bred for disease resistance are just as attractive to

caterpillars, for example, while native cultivars grown for their red leaves are too filled with anthocyanins (pigments that deter feeding) to attract as many caterpillars as straight species (Doug Tallamy, personal communication).

7   For a helpful explanation of plant-fungi relationships, see Greg Rubin and Lucy Warren, *The California Native Landscape* (Portland: Timber Press, 2013).

CHAPTER 2

1   Susan B. Smith and Scott R. McWilliams, "Recommended Plantings for Migratory Songbird Habitat Management," Rochester Institute of Technology RIT Scholar Works, 2015, scholarworks.rit.edu/cgi/viewcontent.cgi?article=1816&context=other.

2   Census estimates are from James B. Nardi, *Life in the Soil: A Guide for Naturalists and Gardeners* (Chicago: University of Chicago Press, 2007). Quantifications of known and unknown species are spotty and conflicting. In *Half Earth: Our Planet's Fight for Life* (New York: Liveright Publishing Corporation, 2016), Edward O. Wilson writes that the number of known species surpassed 2 million in 2015 and that the commonly accepted projection of 8.7 million total plants, animals, algae, fungi, and other eukaryotic microorganisms (those with mitochondria and other organelles) may be an underestimate.

3   The global 2005 Millennium Ecosystem Assessment (millenniumassessment .org) found that 60 percent of the planet's ecosystem services, described as resources that benefit humans, are being degraded or used unsustainably; see Millennium Ecosystem Assessment, *Ecosystems and Human Well-Being: Synthesis* (Washington, DC: Island Press, 2005).

CHAPTER 3

1   See Vera Krischik's research on her faculty page, entomology.umn.edu/faculty-staff/vera-krischik. For more on the chemicals' effects on beetles and other insects, see the Xerces Society report, Hopwood et al., "Beyond the Birds and the Bees: Effects of Neonicotinoid Insecticides on Agriculturally Important Beneficial Invertebrates" (2013).

2   See the abstract of the Netherlands study: Hallmann et al., "Declines in Insectivorous Birds Are Associated with High Neonicotinoid Concentrations," *Nature* (2014): http://dx.doi.org/10.1038/nature13531.

3   Daniel Rubinoff, "Monarch butterfly doesn't need so much help," *Washington Post* (February 20, 2015).

4   Joseph S. Wilson and Olivia Messinger Carril, *The Bees in Your Backyard* (Princeton: Princeton University Press, 2015). The Xerces Society, *Attracting Native Pollinators: Protecting North America's Bees and Butterflies* (North Adams, MA: Storey, 2011).

5   Douglas W. Tallamy, *Bringing Nature Home: How You Can Sustain Wildlife with Native Plants* (Portland: Timber Press, 2007).

6   The National Wildlife Federation's new Native Plant Finder, developed in partnership with the University of Delaware and the US Forest Service, provides a database, searchable by zip code, of region-specific native plants that attract butterflies and moths (see Getting Started). A US region-by-region list that includes information about broader wildlife value per plant species is included in Rick Darke and Doug Tallamy, *The Living Landscape: Designing for Beauty and Biodiversity in the Home Garden* (Portland: Timber Press, 2014).

7   An estimated one-third of pollen-gathering bees in the Eastern United States are specialists, while in the natural desert areas of the Southwest, that figure can be as high as one-half. In many regions the numbers remain unquantified. See Jarrod Fowler, "Specialist Plants of the Northeast: Host Plants and Habitat Conservation," *Northeastern Naturalist*, June 2016.

8   Research has shown that nonnative weedy field borders attract more insects considered problematic to crops, while native plant hedgerows harbor a wide variety of insect predators and parasitoids, in addition to a greater diversity of birds. See Xerces Society, *Farming with Native Beneficial Insects: Ecological Pest Control Solutions* (North Adams, MA: Storey, 2014).

CHAPTER 4

1   A helpful summary of the threats to box turtles is included in John Hadidian, *Wild Neighbors: The Humane Approach to Living with Wildlife* (Washington, DC: Humane Society Press, 2007).

2   Disease transmission findings are described in James S. Adelman, Sahnzi C. Moyers, Damien R. Farine, and Dana M. Hawley, "Feeder use predicts both acquisition and transmission of a contagious pathogen in a North American songbird," *Proceedings of the Royal Society B* (September 15, 2015). Research has found that other unintended consequences of bird feeding can include higher densities of introduced species at the expense of native birds; see Josie A. Galbraith, Jacqueline R. Beggs, Darryl N. Jones, and Margaret C. Stanley, "Supplementary feeding restructures urban bird communities,"

Proceedings of the National Academy of Sciences (January 22, 2015). But some scientists point to research showing positive effects for individual populations; ecologist Joe Smith provides a good summary in "Winter Bird Feeding: Good or Bad for Birds?," *Cool Green Science* (Nature Conservancy blog), January 5, 2015, http://blog.nature.org/science/2015/01/05/winter-bird-feeding-good-or-bad-for-birds/. (I strike a compromise in my own yard, feeding only in the depths of winter when snow blankets the ground and makes it difficult to forage.)

3   J. Amy Belaire et al., "Having Our Yards and Sharing Them, Too: The Collective Effects of Yards on Native Bird Species in an Urban Landscape," *Ecological Applications* (December 2014).

CHAPTER 5

1   *Maryland White-Tailed Deer Plan, 2009–2018*, Maryland Department of Natural Resources, June 2009, http://dnr2.maryland.gov/wildlife/Documents/2009-2018MarylandWTDeerPlan.pdf; J. Scott McDonald and Karl V. Miller, *A History of White-Tailed Deer Restocking in the United States 1878-2004* (Athens, Georgia: D. B. Warnell School of Forest Resources, University of Georgia, 2004).

2   Etienne Benson, "The Urbanization of the Eastern Gray Squirrel in the United States," *Journal of American History* 100, no. 3 (December 2013): 691–710.

3   For fascinating and little-known facts about Lyme disease, see "Lyme Disease," Humane Society of the United States, humanesociety.org/animals/resources/facts/lyme_disease.html.

4   "Invasions of Non-native Earthworms Related to Population Declines of Ground-nesting Songbirds Across a Regional Extent in Northern Hardwood Forests of North America," *Landscape Ecology* 27 (February 2012): 638–96.

5   Professional Wildlife Removal, 2014–2016 Directory of Professionals, http://www.wildlife-removal.com/possumpestcontrol.html.

6   "Aggressive coyotes terrorize northeast neighborhood," *Tucson News Now*, December 16, 2015, http://www.tucsonnewsnow.com/story/30771899/aggressive-coyotes-terrorize-northeast-side-neighborhood; "Geese be gone: Plan calls for dogs to rid Mall of fowl that befoul," *The Washington Post*, March 24, 2015; John Hadidian, "Wildlife in U.S. Cities, Managing Unwanted Animals," *Animals,* November 11, 2015; "Animal control trapping fewer raccoons in Pittsburgh due to new policy," WPXI News 11, June 24, 2015,

http://www.wpxi.com/news/local/animal-control-trapping-fewer-raccoons-pittsburgh-/45989981#__federated=1.

7   See Annie Correal, "Raccoons Invade Brooklyn," *New York Times*, January 1, 2016.

8   Wildlife experts say there's no way to collect the urine from noncaptive wildlife. In-person investigations have confirmed it; one in the 1990s captured sickening images of the animals' pitiful lives, including a particularly haunting one of a fox with his right front leg bone exposed. To feed the animals, the company ground up live hens in wood chippers. (Mary Beth Sweetland, Humane Society of the United States, personal communication.)

9   For detailed instructions and drawings, see "Fence Out Digging Animals," www.humanesociety.org/animals/resources/tips/digging_animals_fence .html.

CHAPTER 6

1   Renée A. Duckworth and Alexander V. Badyaev, "Turf War Twist," *Montana Outdoors* (March–April 2014).

Selected Bibliography

Atkinson, Rob. *Moles.* Stansted, UK: Whittet Books, 2013.

Darke, Rick, and Doug Tallamy. *The Living Landscape: Designing for Beauty and Biodiversity in the Home Garden.* Portland, OR: Timber Press, 2014.

Eaton, Eric R., and Kenn Kaufman. *Field Guide to Insects of North America.* New York: Houghton Mifflin Company, 2007.

Goodrich, Charles, Kathleen Dean Moore, and Frederick J. Swanson. *In the Blast Zone: Catastrophe and Renewal on Mount St. Helens.* Corvallis: Oregon State University Press, 2008.

Hadidian, John. *Wild Neighbors: The Humane Approach to Living with Wildlife.* Washington, DC: The Humane Society of the United States, 2007.

Hartung, Tammi. *The Wildlife-Friendly Vegetable Gardener: How to Grow Food in Harmony with Nature.* North Adams, MA: Storey, 2014.

Haskell, David George. *The Forest Unseen: A Year's Watch in Nature.* New York: Penguin Books, 2012.

Kaufman, Sylvan Ramsey, and Wallace Kaufman. *Invasive Plants: A Guide to Identification, Impacts, and Control of Common North American Species.* Mechanicsburg, PA: Stackpole Books, 2012.

Kimmerer, Robin Wall. *Braiding Sweetgrass: Indigenous Wisdom, Scientific Knowledge, and the Teachings of Plants.* Minneapolis: Milkweed Editions, 2013.

Leister, Mary. *Seasons of Heron Pond.* Owings Mills, MD: Stemmer House, 1981.

———. *Wildlings.* Owings Mills, MD: Stemmer House, 1976.

Mancuso, Stefano, and Alessandra Viola. *Brilliant Green: The Surprising History and Science of Plant Intelligence.* Translated by Joan Benham. Washington, DC: Island Press, 2015. Originally published as *Verde brillante: Sensibilità e intelligenza del mondo vegetale.* Florence: Giunti Editore, 2013.

Nardi, James B. *Life in the Soil: A Guide for Naturalists and Gardeners.* Chicago: The University of Chicago Press, 2007.

Rainer, Thomas, and Claudia West. *Planting in a Post-Wild World: Designing Plant Communities for Resilient Landscapes.* Portland: Timber Press, 2015.

Rubin, Greg, and Lucy Warren. *The California Native Landscape.* Portland: Timber Press, 2013.

Steele, Michael A., and John L. Koprowski. *North American Tree Squirrels.* Washington, DC: Smithsonian Institution, 2001.

Tallamy, Douglas W. *Bringing Nature Home: How You Can Sustain Wildlife with Native Plants.* Portland, OR: Timber Press, 2007.

Wagner, David L. *Caterpillars of Eastern North America.* Princeton: Princeton University Press, 2005.

Wilson, Edward O. *Half Earth: Our Planet's Fight for Life.* New York: Liveright, 2016.

———. *The Meaning of Human Existence.* New York: Liveright, 2014.

Wilson, Joseph S., and Olivia Messinger Carril. *The Bees in Your Backyard.* Princeton: Princeton University Press, 2016.

The Xerces Society, *Attracting Native Pollinators: Protecting North America's Bees and Butterflies.* North Adams, MA: Storey, 2011.

———, *Farming with Native Beneficial Insects.* North Adams, MA: Storey Publishing, 2014.

Acknowledgments

Though I write to help animals, a vast network of people—an ecosystem in itself—makes such work possible. Without Angela Moxley, there would be no Humane Backyard column; she conceived of the bimonthly piece and asked me to write it for *All Animals* magazine. And without the column, which caught the eye of Jennifer Lippert at Princeton Architectural Press, there would be no *Humane Gardener* book. I thank Angela and Jennifer for their creativity and embrace of unconventional ideas.

Each page carries the influence of scientists, naturalists, gardeners, and activists I've had the pleasure of learning from. My interest in compassionate landscaping began during a conversation with John Hadidian in the HSUS lunchroom sixteen years ago. It turned into action with a visit to a native nursery operated by Sara Tangren. And it was validated by the research of Doug Tallamy. They all helped articulate a vocabulary for conveying the concepts I—along with other humane gardeners—already knew in spirit.

Wrapping those thoughts into a book took the superb editing talent of Sara Stemen. She and Simone Kaplan-Senchak helped me purge unnecessary distractions and elevate the book's essence. I couldn't have dreamed of such an arresting design, so I'm glad Ben English did it for me.

For whatever photography skills I possess, I thank Jennifer Beel and Michelle Riley, who imparted the importance of compelling visuals. For images I couldn't capture, I thank those willing to share theirs, especially Jennifer Howard. Identification assistance came from many directions, but no bee question was too small for Olivia Messinger Carril.

Especially generous were friends and reviewers Stephanie Shain and Betsy McFarland. My walking partner, Anne Gellner, gave critical advice at the final hour. Online friends Brandon Smith and Debbie McKevitt were guardian angels, reminding me of the big picture when my world got small.

Loving other species starts with loving our own. I thank my parents for that lesson—and for giving me space to breathe, break the rules, and come home late with mud on my pants.

My husband, Will Heinz, indulged every obsession, patiently absorbing very rough drafts. His eye for detail also led to countless animal rescues, from a katydid caught in the screen to a snapping turtle peeing on him to a goat wandering the street. When I despair at the state of the world, his spirit rescues me too, recalling our power to change that world, one person, one animal, and one thoughtful action at a time.

*All photographs were taken by Nancy Lawson
except for the following:*